Teacher Performance in Bihar, India

DIRECTIONS IN DEVELOPMENT
Human Development

Teacher Performance in Bihar, India
Implications for Education

Shabnam Sinha, Rukmini Banerji, and Wilima Wadhwa

© 2016 International Bank for Reconstruction and Development/The World Bank
1818 H Street NW, Washington, DC 20433
Telephone: 202-473-1000; Internet: www.worldbank.org

Some rights reserved

1 2 3 4   19 18 17 16

This work is a product of the staff of The World Bank with external contributions. The findings, interpretations, and conclusions expressed in this work do not necessarily reflect the views of The World Bank, its Board of Executive Directors, or the governments they represent. The World Bank does not guarantee the accuracy of the data included in this work. The boundaries, colors, denominations, and other information shown on any map in this work do not imply any judgment on the part of The World Bank concerning the legal status of any territory or the endorsement or acceptance of such boundaries.

Nothing herein shall constitute or be considered to be a limitation upon or waiver of the privileges and immunities of The World Bank, all of which are specifically reserved.

Rights and Permissions

This work is available under the Creative Commons Attribution 3.0 IGO license (CC BY 3.0 IGO) http://creativecommons.org/licenses/by/3.0/igo. Under the Creative Commons Attribution license, you are free to copy, distribute, transmit, and adapt this work, including for commercial purposes, under the following conditions:

Attribution—Please cite the work as follows: Sinha, Shabnam, Rukmini Banerji, and Wilima Wadhwa. 2016. *Teacher Performance in Bihar, India: Implications for Education*. Directions in Development. Washington, DC: World Bank. doi:10.1596/978-1-4648-0739-8. License: Creative Commons Attribution CC BY 3.0 IGO

Translations—If you create a translation of this work, please add the following disclaimer along with the attribution: *This translation was not created by The World Bank and should not be considered an official World Bank translation. The World Bank shall not be liable for any content or error in this translation.*

Adaptations—If you create an adaptation of this work, please add the following disclaimer along with the attribution: *This is an adaptation of an original work by The World Bank. Views and opinions expressed in the adaptation are the sole responsibility of the author or authors of the adaptation and are not endorsed by The World Bank.*

Third-party content—The World Bank does not necessarily own each component of the content contained within the work. The World Bank therefore does not warrant that the use of any third-party-owned individual component or part contained in the work will not infringe on the rights of those third parties. The risk of claims resulting from such infringement rests solely with you. If you wish to re-use a component of the work, it is your responsibility to determine whether permission is needed for that re-use and to obtain permission from the copyright owner. Examples of components can include, but are not limited to, tables, figures, or images.

All queries on rights and licenses should be addressed to the Publishing and Knowledge Division, The World Bank, 1818 H Street NW, Washington, DC 20433, USA; fax: 202-522-2625; e-mail: pubrights @worldbank.org.

ISBN (paper): 978-1-4648-0739-8
ISBN (electronic): 978-1-4648-0740-4
DOI: 10.1596/978-1-4648-0739-8

Cover photo: © Pratham. Used with permission; further permission required for reuse.
Cover design: Debra Naylor, Naylor Design, Inc.

Library of Congress Cataloging-in-Publication Data has been requested

Contents

Foreword   *ix*
Acknowledgements   *xi*
About the Authors   *xiii*
Abbreviations   *xv*

	Executive Summary	1
Chapter 1	**Who Are the Teachers?**	13
	Introduction	13
	General Information about Teachers	13
	Educational Qualifications and Training	18
	Working in School: Activities and Attitudes	21
	Conclusion	25
	Notes	25
Chapter 2	**What Are Classrooms Like?**	27
	Introduction	27
	Classroom Organization and Classroom Environment	28
	Classroom and Teaching Activities	34
	Teacher-Student Interaction	36
	Conclusion	37
	Notes	37
	Reference	38
Chapter 3	**Teacher Assessments**	39
	Introduction	39
	Teacher Questionnaire and Teacher Assessment: Math	41
	Teacher Questionnaire and Teacher Assessment: Language	54
	Thoughts on a Way Forward	63
	Notes	65
Chapter 4	**Generating Composite Scores for Teacher Capability for Teaching**	67
	Introduction	67
	Generating Composite Scores	67

	Teacher Characteristics and Composite Scores	70
	Looking Ahead	72
	Notes	73

Figures

1.1	Educational Qualification of Teachers	19
1.2	Educational Qualification, by Teacher Type	19
1.3	Educational Qualification of Teachers, by Age	20
3.1	Sample Response: Can Teachers Do Division with All the Steps?	42
3.2	Can Teachers Learn from Children's Mistakes?	44
3.3	Sample Incorrect Response: Do Teachers Know BODMAS?	46
3.4	Sample Correct Response: Do Teachers Know BODMAS?	47
3.5	Sample Correct Response: Can Teachers Show How to Do Calculations for Perimeter?	48
3.6	Sample Response: Can Teachers Show How a Percentage Problem Is to Be Done?	50
3.7	Developing Questions for Children Based on Context	51
3.8	Sample Incorrect Response: Teacher Does Not Use Mathematical Operations	52
3.9	Sample Incorrect Response: Teacher Is Unable to Construct a Logical and Realistic Scenario	52
3.10	Sample Incorrect Response: Teacher Uses Mathematically Inappropriate Numbers	52
3.11	Data Table and Interpretation Task	53
3.12	Do Teachers Know Grammar?	55
3.13	Sample Response: Punctuation Question	57
3.14	Sample Response: Correcting Children's Work: Reading Comprehension	58
3.15	Sample Response: Vocabulary	59
3.16	Question Development Task	60

Tables

1.1	Teacher Distribution, by School Type	14
1.2	Type of Teachers	14
1.3	Type of Teacher, by School Type	14
1.4	Age Distribution, by Teacher Type	14
1.5	Age Distribution of Teachers, by School Type	15
1.6	Gender Distribution, by Age of Teacher	15
1.7	Teachers, by Caste	15
1.8	Teachers Whose Children Attend Government or Private Schools	16
1.9	Teacher Types, by Location of Residence	16
1.10	Teachers' Commute Time to School	16
1.11	Teachers' Supplemental Work, by Type and Gender	17

1.12	Years Teaching since Appointment, by Teacher Type	17
1.13	Years in Current School, by Teacher Type	17
1.14	Transfers by Teacher Type	18
1.15	Professional Qualifications of Teachers	20
1.16	Days of Teacher Training, 2012–13	20
1.17	Training Feedback	21
1.18	Distribution of Teachers by Classes (Grades) and Average Number of Subjects per Class	22
1.19	Time Teachers Spent on Activities per Week	22
1.20	Hardest Class (Grade) to Teach, by Teacher Type	23
1.21	Who Guides the Teachers?	23
1.22	Time Spent on Teacher Activities	23
1.23	Teachers' Opinions	24
2.1	Total Number of Classroom Visits, 2013–14	28
2.2	Location of Observed Classes, Upper Primary Schools	29
2.3	Incidence of Multigrade Classes, Class IV	29
2.4	Incidence of Multigrade Classes in Observed Schools in Bihar, Class VI	30
2.5	Multigrade Classrooms for Class IV by School Type, Visit 1	30
2.6	Monograde in All Three Visits, Upper Primary Schools	31
2.7	Multigrade Classes by Number of Teachers in the School, Class IV	31
2.8	Multigrade Classes by Number of Teachers in the School, Class VI	31
2.9	Classroom Infrastructure, Total of Three Visits	32
2.10	Classroom Infrastructure by School Type, Visit 1, Class IV	33
2.11	Timetable Indicators	33
2.12	Variation in Teaching Activities	35
2.13	Teacher–Student Interactions: Positive Activities	37
3.1	Framework for Mathematics Assessment	41
3.2	Teachers' Ability to Identify Children's Mistakes	42
3.3	Teachers' Ability to Solve Division Problem with Steps	43
3.4	Teachers' Ability to Identify Correct Statements about Children's Work	45
3.5	Teachers' Ability to Solve Step-by-Step Process of Numerical Computation (BODMAS)	47
3.6	Teachers' Ability to Solve Perimeter Problem Step by Step and in Sequence	49
3.7	Teachers' Ability to Solve Percentage Problem Step by Step and in Sequence	50
3.8	Teachers' Ability to Complete Data Interpretation Task Correctly	53
3.9	Framework for Assessment of Teaching of Language (Hindi)	54
3.10	Teachers' Ability to Correct Children's Mistakes: Grammar and Sentence Construction	56
3.11	Teachers' Ability to Correct Children's Grammar and Sentence Construction	56
3.12	Teachers' Ability to Correct Children's Mistakes: Punctuation	57

3.13	Teachers' Ability to Correct Children's Mistakes: Punctuation	57
3.14	Teachers' Ability to Correct Reading Comprehension Questions	59
3.15	Teachers' Ability to Explain Difficult Words in Simple Language	59
3.16	Teachers' Ability to Create Clear and Appropriate Questions	61
3.17	Teachers' Ability to Summarize Content	62
4.1	Composition of Teacher Assessment Language Score	68
4.2	Composition of Teacher Assessment Math Score	69
4.3	Distribution of Composite Scores	70
4.4	Teacher Scores, by Gender	71
4.5	Teacher Scores, by Caste	71
4.6	Teacher Scores, by Education Category	71
4.7	Teacher Scores, by Professional Qualifications	71
4.8	Teacher Scores, by Years of Experience as Teacher	72
4.9	Teacher Scores, by Whether They Have Taught in a Private School in the Past	72

Foreword

India is uniquely positioned to help end extreme poverty by 2030 and boost shared prosperity in the world. India's growth in gross domestic product of (current US$ billion) 2,049[1] makes it a lower-middle-income country, but its development challenges are deep and complex despite significant achievements made over the past decades. Between 2005 and 2010, 53 million people were lifted out of poverty. Progress on human development has been remarkable; life expectancy more than doubled, from 31 years in 1947 to 65 years in 2012, and adult literacy more than quadrupled, from 18 percent in 1951 to 74 percent in 2011. However, about 60 percent of India's population of more than 200 million lives in low-income and special category states[2] where poverty rates are close to 40 percent. In Bihar, more than half the state's population of 100.3 million are poor. The state has a large rural population: only slightly more than 11 percent of Bihar's population lives in urban areas.

The overarching objective of the World Bank Group's support to India and its low-income states is to support poverty reduction and shared prosperity. With a young population and 8 million people entering the labor force every year, India could reap a substantial demographic dividend, but there could also be considerable stress if employment opportunities are not commensurate with expectations. As India ranks 135 on the Human Development Index as of 2014, promoting human development and strengthening social programs are crucial to economic integration and inclusive growth; these goals require better accountability arrangements with incentives and community participation for enhancing service delivery. A focus on learning outcomes is warranted across all levels of education with the role of teachers highlighted as a major determinant of quality. To have systemic or transformational impact, teacher education needs to innovate and pilot new approaches, introducing innovative financing instruments for leveraging resources. The Enhancing Teacher Effectiveness in Bihar SURE program, with its use of results-based financing and use of new ICTs, and its focus on professional development and teacher performance tracking, is the World Bank's new effort in this sector.

Lack of information on teachers and teacher education institutions limits what decision makers can do to plan and project future training needs. Efforts to improve teacher management are also constrained by a lack of clear standards for benchmarking teacher performance. The Enhancing Teacher Effectiveness program has initiated the development of a set of teacher standards and competencies that have helped establish a baseline database for teacher performance. Indicators measure teacher performance in three key domains: subject knowledge, teacher practices, and time-on-task. These are expected to inform preservice and in-service professional development programs. The study presents interesting facts about what teachers are like (their profiles); what they believe (teacher attitudes and perceptions); what classrooms are like (single grade versus multigrade); the quality of classroom instruction and lastly and most importantly, what teachers know. The study includes one of the largest samples in the world on teacher assessment, covering 400 schools and more than 2,000 teachers over two academic years.

Through appropriate testing mechanisms, assessment of teacher capability and key skills commonly used in teaching and final scores show that it is indeed time for urgent corrective actions to ensure improved teacher competencies in Bihar. The study found that the language score (on a scale of 0–10) had a mean of about 4.5, or less than 50 percent. The mean math score (on a scale of 0–12) stood at 7, or about 58 percent. The scores are a startling revelation that much more needs to be done in the teacher education space to strengthen teacher performance with a series of outcome-oriented reform strategies.

This study has immense relevance for teacher education programs at the global level, reflecting the need for periodically monitoring teacher performance and eventually incentivizing good performance. Tracking the effect of investments in the education sector on teacher behavior and performance would help generate robust feedback loops that can be built in to training programs to synchronize teacher training with teacher needs for improved teacher performance. The tools can be enhanced for more sophisticated use at the national level in India and in countries with similar teacher education profiles for improving teacher accountability.

I hope this study and publication are useful for policy makers, educational functionaries, and teacher educators to identify the training needs of teachers by devising and using teacher performance indicators and modalities that are simple, understandable, and can be used by teacher educators at decentralized levels in collaboration with community stakeholders.

Claudia Costin
Senior Director, Education
The World Bank Group

Notes

1. Submitted by the World Bank for Unified Survey India, fiscal year 2014/15.
2. Low-income states are defined as those below US$494 gross state domestic product per capita, and special category states consist mostly of northern mountainous states, which are sparsely populated, and those with high transport costs, leading to high delivery costs for public services. World Bank Group Country Partnership Strategy for India, 2013–17.

Acknowledgements

The task team consisted of Shabnam Sinha, Task Team Leader, with Fabian Toegel, Sangeeta Dey, Muna Meky, and Toby Linden. This study was commissioned by the World Bank as a part of its preparatory work on a project on India, Enhancing Teacher Effectiveness in Bihar, and was conducted by the ASER Centre, the research and assessment arm of Pratham, a large nongovernmental organization in India. The study's team was led by Rukmini Banerji, Wilima Wadhwa, and Ranajit Bhattacharyya, and others.

The authors thank the Education Department of the Bihar state government and the State Council of Educational Research and Training, not only for suggestions and comments during the design phase, but also for their interest and engagement in interpreting and discussing the preliminary results. Finally, a huge debt of gratitude to the schools, teachers, and children who participated wholeheartedly in the study. Without their support and cooperation, this study could not have happened.

About the Authors

Rukmini Banerji is Director of the ASER Centre, the research and assessment unit of Pratham. Since 1996, Banerji has been with Pratham, one of India's largest NGOs working in education (www.pratham.org). She has led the Annual Status of Education Report (ASER) effort since it was launched in 2005. ASER has been acknowledged nationally and internationally for its innovative model of household-based, citizen-led assessment that has impacted education policy and practice within India and has been adapted for use in several countries in Africa and Asia. In 2008, Banerji was awarded the Maulana Abul Kalam Shiksha Puraskar by the government of Bihar, India. Over the years, she has represented Pratham and the ASER Centre in various national and international forums and is a member of committees in India and abroad. Rukmini writes frequently on education for Hindi and English dailies in India and enjoys writing books and stories for children.

Shabnam Sinha is Senior Education and Institutional Development Specialist at the World Bank in the India Country Office. She leads the World Bank's India program on universalization of elementary education, the Sarva Shiksha Abhiyan, one of the largest elementary sector programs in the world. She works on secondary education and teacher education programs at the World Bank. She leads the Enhancing Teacher Effectiveness in Bihar project, which supports a "financing for results" approach. She also works on India's skills development and vocational education programs through public-private partnerships. The India Country Assistance Strategy provides special developmental support to low-income states in the country; through it, Sinha is in charge of the state of Bihar, helping multi-sectoral teams in effective implementation and monitoring of Bank-wide programs in the state. Before joining the World Bank, Sinha was chief executive officer for a public-private partnership (PPP) in education for a large private sector company. Sinha's assignment included setting up the portfolio of the PPP in education, including PPP frameworks in coordination with governments in school education, teacher training, and skills development. She was senior program management specialist (education) with the United States Agency for International Development (USAID). In a career spanning more than 23 years, she has also worked at the National Council of Educational Research and Training, the national academic authority in India that works on school education and teacher training.

Wilima Wadhwa is the Director of the ASER Centre. She has been associated with ASER since its inception in 2005 and is the architect of the ASER survey and other primary research studies currently being undertaken by the ASER Centre. ASER's unique approach to measuring learning outcomes has been recognized nationally and internationally and has also been adapted by several other countries in Asia and Africa.

Wadhwa earned her undergraduate degree, with honors in economics, from Delhi University; MA degrees in economics from Delhi University and the University of California; and a PhD in economics from the University of California.

Wadhwa has been published extensively and teaches statistics and econometrics at the University of California (Irvine), and the Indian Statistical Institute (New Delhi). She has also been a member of various government and international committees, including the Questionnaire Expert Group for Program for International Student Assessment (PISA-D). Wadhwa's other research interests include development and economics of education.

Abbreviations

BITE	Block Institute of Teacher Education
BODMAS	Brackets, Orders (powers and roots), Division and Multiplication, Addition, and Subtraction
BRC	Block Resource Center
CCE	Continuous Comprehensive Evaluation
CRC	Cluster Resource Center
CTE	College of Teacher Education
DIET	District Institute of Education and Training
EVS	environmental studies
GoI	government of India
IASE	Institute for Advanced Learning in Education
ICDS	Integrated Child Development Services
MHRD	Ministry of Human Resource Development
NCERT	National Council of Educational Research and Training
NCF	National Curriculum Framework
NCFTE	National Curriculum Framework of Teacher Education
NCTE	National Council of Teacher Education
NUEPA	National University of Educational Planning and Administration
OBC	Other Backward Classes
PTR	pupil-teacher ratio
RTE	Right of Children to Free and Compulsory Education Act
SC	Scheduled Castes
SCERT	State Council of Educational Research and Training
SSA	Sarva Shiksha Abhiyan
ST	Scheduled Tribes
TET	Teacher Eligibility Test
TTI	teacher training institution

Executive Summary

Background

Teacher Education in India

For preservice training, the National Council of Teacher Education (NCTE), a statutory body at the federal level, is responsible for planned and coordinated development of teacher education in India. The NCTE lays down norms and standards for various teacher education courses; minimum qualifications for teacher educators; course and content and duration; and minimum qualification for entry of student teachers into various courses. It also grants recognition to institutions (government, government-aided, and self-financing) interested in undertaking such courses including private sector institutions. In general, the public service commission of the respective states undertakes teacher recruitment at the state level.[1]

For in-service training, the country has a large network of government-owned teacher training institutions (TTIs). At the federal level, the National Council of Educational Research and Training (NCERT), along with its regional institutes, prepares materials for various teacher training courses and undertakes training of teachers and teacher educators. The National University of Educational Planning and Administration (NUEPA) also provides institutional support on teacher management efforts.

The Colleges of Teacher Education (CTEs) and Institutes for Advanced Learning in Education (IASEs) provide in-service training to secondary and senior secondary school teachers and teacher educators. At the district level, in-service training is provided by the District Institutes of Education and Training (DIETs). The Block Resource Centers (BRCs) and Cluster Resource Centers (CRCs)—the subdistrict-level institutional structures under Sarva Shiksha Abhiyan (SSA), India's program for the universalization of elementary education—form the decentralized-level institutions for providing in-service training and on-site support of school teachers.

For preservice training, the government and government-aided teacher education institutions are financially supported by the respective state governments. Through a national scheme for teacher education, the federal government supports more than 930 institutions, including DIETs, CTEs, IASEs, and the Block Institutes of Teacher Training (BITEs). For in-service training, financial support is largely provided by the SSA, which is the main vehicle for implementation of the "right" in the Right of Children to Free and Compulsory Education Act (RTE Act), 2009. Under the SSA, school teachers are provided a 20-day in-service training; untrained teachers receive a 60-day refresher course; and freshly trained recruits have a 30-day orientation.

The NCTE prepared the National Curriculum Framework of Teacher Education (NCFTE) in 2009 to support implementation of the RTE Act and consistent with the school curriculum as prepared under the NCF-2005. The framework underscores the following tenets for teacher education:

- Reflective practice should be the central aim of teacher education.
- Student teachers should be provided the opportunity for self-learning, reflection, assimilation, and articulation of new ideas.
- Student teachers should be provided the opportunity to develop capacities of self-directed learning and the abilities to think, be critical, and work in groups.
- Student teachers should be provided the opportunity to observe and engage with children and communicate with and relate to children.

The framework specified the broad areas of study in theoretical and practical domains, curricular transaction, and assessment strategies for teacher education programs. The framework has identified the approach and methodology of in-service teacher training programs.

Teacher Education in Bihar

Bihar's economic growth averaged 13 percent for fiscal years 2005–06 and 2009–10; this was higher than the national growth rate of 8.2 percent. The state remains crucial to India's overall progress on making growth more inclusive. Only 61.8 percent of Bihar's population is literate (males, 71.2 percent and females, 51.5 percent). As per the 2014 figures released by the Integrated Child Development Services (ICDS), 50 percent of Bihar's children are malnourished. Bihar's maternal mortality ratio remains low, with 261 women per 100,000 live births dying. In 2009 the government of India (GoI) set an ambitious goal to improve access to and quality of education through the RTE Act. The RTE Act prescribed strict standards and norms that all schools are required to meet. Standards include (a) free elementary education to all children aged six to 14; (b) provision of appropriate infrastructure and learning material for all schools; and (c) a pupil-teacher ratio (PTR) of 30:1 at the primary level and 35:1 at the upper primary level by 2015, with all teachers meeting minimum professional qualifications.

These reforms saw success in improving education inputs in Bihar. Previously Bihar was characterized by a severe lack of pedagogical resources and infrastructure in primary education, as evidenced by low attendance rates (77.8 percent), substantial numbers of out-of-school children (181,086), and a very high PTR (76:1)—one of the highest in India. Under the SSA program, the main vehicle for RTE's implementation, Bihar has seen an increase in access rates, a significant increase in comprehensive classroom infrastructure, and reduced PTRs. However, Bihar is still grappling with significant challenges in improving the quality of education.

The 2014 National Achievement Survey shows that Bihar ranks second from the bottom in the list of states in students' learning achievement both in languages and mathematics.

International evidence suggests that once children enter school, the single most important determinant of learning is teacher performance, and its benefits are expected to translate into national economic gains. Estimating the economic value of higher teacher quality in the United States, Hanushek, Link, and Woessmann (2011) found that a teacher who is one standard deviation above mean teacher effectiveness would generate annual marginal gains of US$400,000 in terms of the present value of future student earnings—and potentially more when other conditions change. The authors also suggest that replacing the bottom 5–8 percent of teachers with "average-quality" teachers could move the United States to near the top in international rankings in mathematics and science achievement (Hanushek, Link, and Woessmann 2011). While no such calculations exist for India, a recent regional study on education quality in South Asia reported that the economic value of better teacher quality is bound to be large because the role of teachers is magnified when children are first-generation schoolgoers and home inputs are limited (Dundar et al. 2014).

Through the massive hiring of about 300,000 contract teachers, Bihar almost doubled the number of teachers in elementary schools from 2006 to 2013, leading to a reduction in the pupil-teacher ratio (PTR) as needed under RTE. For reduced PTRs to translate into improved learning outcomes, it is critical that robust systems for developing high-quality teachers are in place. However, the recent expansion in the number of teachers, compounded by years of underinvestment since the 1990s in teacher programs, has led to a teaching workforce characterized by low academic content, ineffectual teaching practices, unacceptable levels of absenteeism, and outdated monitoring and governance arrangements.

What Is Needed for Teacher Education Reform in Bihar?

Exigent to teacher reform in Bihar are key actions needed for strengthening teacher education institutions through sustainable, innovative, cost-effective scale-up mechanisms to increase the supply of quality trained teachers. Support mechanisms to improve classroom effectiveness and pedagogy, including the training needs of teachers, require benchmarking of their competencies to understand the deficiencies to prepare effective strategies for building their capacities. Enhancing school leadership support plays a vital role in enlisting and guiding the talents and energies of teachers, pupils, and parents toward achieving common educational aims. A school principal has many tasks, including finances, managing teachers, and engaging communities and parents in the education system.

Inadequate incentive mechanisms—including entry-level teacher pay and unappealing working conditions for talented candidates—have led to gaps in teacher motivation. Bihar has slowly begun strengthening capacity at the district, block, and school levels. According to a recent study, Bihar experienced a 10 percent reduction in absenteeism rates between 2003 and 2010 as a result of improved inspection and monitoring (Muralidharan et al. 2014). However, low rates of teacher time-on-task[2] are still major problems in education service delivery, and teacher absenteeism is as high as 20 percent. Lack of teacher performance benchmarks has made it virtually impossible for the state teacher education system to be able to track the impact of teacher development and management efforts on teacher performance and to link teacher evaluations to career development.

Institutional linkages from the state to district and subdistrict levels for planning, monitoring, and management of teachers are deficient. Strong administrative and governance mechanisms would help effective teacher management and monitoring to link data on teachers with their training and professional development. Policy makers and teacher educators need access to information to track and plan their teacher development and training strategy.

The number of certified teachers in Bihar is still lower than what is required for an effective learning environment. Bihar has very few training institutions. The state's combined current training capacity of all such institutions is less than 5,000 newly trained teachers per year. Bihar needs to train at least 10 times more teachers annually than existing capacities; by 2020 the total number of teachers is expected to exceed 600,000. Because of a flattened salary trajectory and varying educational backgrounds, these teachers, plus others already in the system, require continuous support to improve their effectiveness in the classroom. Many teachers lack the capacity to teach the subjects required owing to the lowering of qualification thresholds for teachers. This leaves a large portion of the teacher workforce with inadequate knowledge content and ineffective teaching practices.

Preparing Teacher Competency Benchmarks

Through its recently approved project *Enhancing Teacher Effectiveness in Bihar*, the World Bank will be supporting the state with a US$250 million loan to improve the effectiveness of elementary school teachers. The project aims at enhancing the effectiveness of school teachers in Bihar at the elementary level (Classes I–VIII). The project will help the system of teacher education equip teachers with the necessary skills and knowledge to be more effective in the classroom and will support enhanced accountability measures for improved governance. The project is a unique opportunity to enhance teacher effectiveness by creating robust systemwide improvements focused on instructional excellence. The project focuses on (a) developing high-quality teacher education institutions for improved program delivery; (b) enabling certification of unqualified elementary school teachers and their continuous professional development; (c) developing an effective teacher management system with a robust monitoring and evaluation mechanism; (d) improving accountability mechanisms at the school level; and (e) improving financial and governance mechanisms.

The project required the creation of teacher accountability and teacher performance benchmarks against which teachers' performance could be measured. The present study was undertaken as a World Bank and Bihar government collaborative initiative to assess teacher performance, classroom instruction processes, and time-on-task. These inputs and index-based scores of teacher performance will feed into and inform the development of the training strategy. The scores will provide usable data and information that can be embedded in and improve preservice and in-service teacher professional development programs.

The Study

The World Bank requisitioned ASER Centre—the assessment, survey, evaluation, and research arm of Pratham, an Indian NGO—for conducting this survey. The study was undertaken by factoring in suggestions and comments of the Education Department of the government of Bihar and of SCERT during the design and implementation phase.

Given the ambitious scope and scale of the interventions aimed both at increasing the quantity and quality of teachers in the system, it was important to develop methods and measures to provide timely information about whether intended objectives were being achieved. The development of contextually relevant and useful indicators of teacher performance early in this process of reform was taken up so that there would be useful information for planners and policy makers about the areas in which progress was satisfactory and those which needed additional attention.

This study of teachers and teaching in Bihar explores a set of interrelated factors that influence how teachers teach. It was designed as a series of data collection exercises, conducted between July 2013 and December 2014. Four hundred schools and more than 2,000 teachers were tracked during three visits to each school. The study used a variety of methods, including teacher surveys; classroom and school observations; and an assessment of teachers' subject matter knowledge, ability to communicate, and ability to learn from children's work. Observations of a randomly selected group of schools, teachers, and students from four districts in Bihar enabled analyses linking teacher attributes, teaching practices, school and classroom organization, and teachers' capability to teach to build a composite picture of teachers and teaching in Bihar today.

The findings generated by the study provide significant inputs and suggestions for designing future teacher training and teacher professional development in Bihar. This research potentially has utility not only in India but more widely.

Summary of Research Findings
What Are Teachers Like?

Even a quick glance at the background information of teachers in Bihar underscores the urgent need for major investment in teacher quality in the state. More than 2,000 teachers in 400 randomly sampled schools in four districts participated in the study. Of these, only a quarter were regular teachers. Close to 60 percent of the teachers in the study were less than 30 years old, and more than 75 percent of the teachers surveyed had been teaching for 10 years or less. About half the teachers who participated in the study did not have any professional qualifications for teaching. Almost two-thirds of the teachers surveyed had not attended even one in-service training in the fiscal year (2012–13) preceding this study.

What Do Teachers Believe?

To explore teacher attitudes and perceptions, teachers were asked whether they agreed with certain statements. They were asked to mark their response on a scale of strongly agree to strongly disagree. These statements covered a variety of topics, ranging from pedagogical practices to their opinions about parents and children. For example, 96 percent of teachers agreed with the statement "I always make a lesson plan before teaching a class." Eighty-two percent of teachers said that they made a lesson plan quite often. Similarly, 88 percent of teachers agreed with the statement that they made their students work in groups in class. And 81 percent said that they do that quite often. About 85 percent of teachers agreed with the statement that they knew the names of all their students.

Do teachers' perceptions align with the reality of their teaching context? Some of the responses are worth highlighting here. For example, 86 percent of teachers agreed that "most children in Class IV in my school can do subtraction" and "all children in Class IV in this school can read fluently." None of the student data corroborates this belief. A majority of teachers believed that the textbooks are not too difficult for children and that their main objective as a teacher is to finish the syllabus. More than half of all teachers agreed that if children do not learn well, it is the responsibility of the parents. Almost all teachers stated that the school does everything to help a child to learn well, and half of all teachers argued that to do well students need private tuition in addition to regular school.

One of the key objectives of future teacher training and professional development must be to enable teachers to see the realities underlying teaching learning in their schools and to make them understand and accept the responsibility of ensuring that children learn.

What Are Classrooms Like?

An important part of this study focuses on life in two grades—Class IV and Class VI—in two types of government schools: those with only primary grades (Classes I to V) and those with primary and upper primary classes (Classes I to VIII). The following issues emerge:

High Incidence of Multigrade Classrooms. With large numbers of teachers entering the education system in the last ten years and with an expansion in infrastructure, the common perception is that the incidence of multigrade groupings has decreased considerably. Repeated classroom observations during the course of this study noted that multigrade groupings are more common in primary grades (such as Class IV) as compared with grades at the upper primary level (such as Class VI) even in the same school. In the upper primary schools, close to 60 percent of all Class VI classes that were observed were single grade while only 44 percent or so Class IV classes sat by themselves. But the comparison of Class IV classes in the two types of schools found that only 14 percent of Class IV classes in primary schools sat by themselves as compared with 44 percent of monograde Class IV classes in the upper primary schools.

Despite improvements over time in the availability of teachers at the school level, it is still worth noting that significantly large proportions of Class IV and Class VI classes are taught with other grades in the same classroom. If this continues to be the reality of schools in Bihar, then the government needs to ensure that elementary school teachers are adequately equipped to deal with multigrade contexts and well supported through on-site visits and monitoring. The study suggests that more effective ways of organizing classes need to be systematically explored. Given that schools still do not have adequate numbers of teachers, how classes are to be grouped for teaching and how to sustain appropriate groupings over time are issues that need attention.

Traditional Teaching and Classroom Activities. Overall, the data show that teaching in Bihar's elementary schools is carried out in a traditional way. Students sit in rows and work individually. There is hardly any group work. The observations of classroom interactions in both grades—Class IV and Class VI—indicate that the teaching was almost entirely driven by textbook content. Most teachers were observed to be reading from the textbook (89 percent) and asking oral questions to students from the textbook (67 percent) or asking students to recite (49 percent). Fifty-seven percent of teachers were observed writing on the blackboard—usually content from the textbook—and in 44 percent of the classes, students were asked to write (in their notebooks or slates). Hardly any material other than textbooks were used—either by teachers or students.

Gap between Talk and Action. There seem to be substantial differences between what was self-reported by teachers and what they were observed to be doing in a classroom: 78.6 percent of teachers reported that they often use teaching learning materials (TLM) other than textbooks during a class. However, classroom observations do not suggest that this is the case. In less than 17 percent of classrooms was any material other than textbooks visible. At least half the teachers said that they use activities other than what is suggested in the textbook. But such practices were rarely seen when classrooms were being observed. More than 80 percent of teachers said they encourage their children to work in groups. Again, this was hardly ever seen in the classroom observation time.

The gap between talk and action suggests that teachers know what should be done but are unable to get it done. Teachers seem to know what elements of good teaching are (for example, organizing group work, assigning tasks to students to do on their own, contextualizing tasks, or using a variety of materials) but are unable to actually do it in their classroom. A clear implication of this discrepancy is that when teachers are being trained (in-service or preservice) a great deal of attention has to be paid to demonstrate and help teachers to translate theoretical concepts into practice. Knowing about "child-centered" pedagogy is not helpful unless the teachers are actually able to do it.

What Do Teachers Know?

All teachers in the elementary schools sampled for the study were asked to participate in a pen and paper assessment. The framework used in the assessment of teacher capability for teaching was based broadly on three kinds of skills that are commonly used in teaching. This includes the ability of teachers to do the following:

- Understand children by looking at their work (in arithmetic and in language—Hindi).
- Explain content and processes (for example, texts and vocabulary in language and operations, processes, and problems in math).
- Create questions and examples that are context specific and related to the everyday life of children.

Most of the tasks that the teachers were asked to do in the questionnaire and assessment were common activities expected to be seen in a typical Indian elementary school classroom. The evidence from the study suggests the following points may be useful to keep in mind while designing preservice and in-service training modules for teachers.[3]

Subject Matter Basic Knowledge Needs Strengthening for Some. As part of the assessment, teachers were given very basic kinds of tasks (for example, in math they were asked to solve a long division problem, show correct use of brackets and operations, compute percentages, or calculate area). All of these are math problems from primary grades. Depending on the question, anywhere between three-quarters to two-thirds of the teachers could do the question correctly. Similarly in language. The others who are weak in basic skills or in basic concepts need to be identified early in their career (either at the preservice stage or soon after) and given the necessary help and support. It is wrong to assume that all teachers have basic language or math skills. In the recruitment process, the testing can be focused on ensuring that the incoming or selected teachers are beyond this basic level.

Weak in Translating Content and Processes into Practice. A key part of any teacher's work is to be able to help children access content or enable them to build skills in a manner that they are able to comprehend and engage. Knowing how to translate "teaching" into "learning" for all children is essential. Here is an example: while almost 78 percent of teachers could do a long division (3-digit by 1-digit) problem correctly, when it came to explaining the correct steps to solve a division problem, only 10.5 percent of the teachers got all the steps right.

Similarly there is a huge gap in the case of solving a percentage problem and explaining the correct steps to solve the problem. For example, in the case of having to solve a percentage problem, 64.1 percent of teachers could answer the question correctly, but only 15.1 percent got the right answer and also showed the correct and complete steps to reach the answer.

The ability to explain in ways accessible to children is a critical component of effective teaching. Even in a typical, traditional Indian elementary school classroom, it is expected that the teacher will be able to comprehensively and correctly explain the concept being taught and lay out step by step the processes or the operations that the child has to learn. Most textbooks contain examples of such explanations. However, data from this study suggest that a large number of teachers need help in providing complete, correct, and comprehensive explanations to children. Therefore, in training it may be worth reinforcing exactly how basic operations are to be taught and if possible practice these explanations in the presence of faculty or master trainers.

Need to Learn about Children from Correcting Their Work. A close look at the work done by children helps in understanding not only whether a concept or a skill needs to be revised or strengthened or even taught again to the group but also points to which children need additional help and on what. Common mistakes highlight common problems, and individual mistakes point to specific help needed by specific children.

Examples of children's work, especially by children who have been able to move beyond the boundaries of what was expected of them, can also help the teacher to move the teaching in the class in different directions.

Typically teachers spend a considerable part of their time in correcting children's work. Yet questions in this study that asked teachers to think about what they learned from looking at children's work were not easy for them to answer. For example, teachers were shown examples of students' written work and asked to identify mistakes in spelling and grammar. In the particular case, there were three mistakes; close to half the teachers could only identify one mistake; and one-third could not identify any mistakes. This and other evidence suggest that it would be pertinent to collect and use samples of children's work (both from academically good and weaker students) as part of teacher training modules. This can be done in each subject and as part of the teaching of any concept during the teacher training. Such samples could be purposively chosen to prepare teachers to learn from children's work.

Overall, the findings from the study strongly suggest that teacher training modules should integrate children's work with the core content in a systematic way. This will strengthen teacher preparation and professional development and prepare teachers for the actual ground-level realities they face or will face in the classroom.

Contextualizing Teaching to Connect to Children's Everyday Lives and Knowledge. The NCF-2005 stresses the need to be able to connect what is happening in the classroom to children's life outside the classroom. Teachers' ability to do this is a key component of good teaching. In the study, the teacher assessment had a few tasks that required teachers to either devise word problems in math or create different types of questions in language using local information. The ability to formulate both questions from numbers and language is a particular problem for the teachers. Over one-third of them correctly formulated a fact retrieval question from a simple given situation, and just about one-third of them could create an inference-based question. Many teachers did not perform well in these tasks. Therefore, any teacher training module should incorporate practice of how this contextualization of teaching is to be done, especially if it is to be done meaningfully to connect with children, their lives, and their prior knowledge.

Teacher Scores and Teacher Characteristics. It is often thought that teachers with higher qualifications will be able to teach better. In fact the RTE Act lays down norms for educational standards that teachers must meet. In terms of average scores (based on basic subject matter knowledge) in Hindi and arithmetic, teachers with higher educational qualifications score slightly higher. However it is also the case that scores need to be higher across the distribution of teacher qualifications. The relationship between years of teaching or professional qualifications and teacher scores is much more mixed. If the composition of the composite teacher score moves beyond subject matter knowledge to other aspects of teaching, the differences between different kinds of teachers may become even less clear.

Final Scores. The language score lies on a scale of 0–10 and the math score 0–12. The mean language score was 4.46, which is less than 50 percent. The mean math score was higher, at 7 out of a maximum of 12. The average score of teachers in language stood at 44.6 percent and 58.3 percent in mathematics.

The Way Forward

As more and more teachers join schools and as more investments are made in teacher training and professional development, it is hoped that these would lead to improved classroom interactions and practices especially if training is targeted at changing some of the traditional teaching behavior that is commonly seen in Bihar's schools. The points raised in the previous section have a variety of implications for teacher preparation. If we want classroom practices to become more interactive—with less teacher- or textbook-driven and more oriented toward group work—then preservice and in-service teacher training must incorporate training on these elements in the new modules that are being developed. Discussions around videotaped classroom sessions could also be a way in which classroom practices are brought into teacher training sessions, both in general and with respect to specific subjects.

The current study looked at a variety of dimensions of teachers and teaching to provide a comprehensive view of a "baseline" stage in Bihar. Periodic followup studies can be done to provide a feedback loop into the content and delivery of the ongoing teacher training programs. It is important that such feedback loops are built into training programs so that the process evolves in sync with the needs of the teachers. The current classroom observation format was designed to generate such information and the observation formats can be used as template that could be further enhanced for more sophisticated use, based on the level of training of the observers.

Notes

1. Teacher Education Department, Ministry of Human Resource Development, Government of India.
2. The actual amount of focused engagement and time spent by teachers on instructional processes and teaching.
3. In collaboration with the Bihar government and UNICEF, the ASER Centre/Pratham conducted a state-level student achievement study in every district in Bihar in May 2014. Many of the areas in which student performance was poor are the same as those in which the teachers were found to be weak in the present study. Hence, the suggestions in this document also draw from the results from other studies.

References

Dundar, H., T. Beteille, M. Riboud, and A. Deolikar. 2014. *Student Learning in South Asia: Challenges, Opportunities, and Policy Priorities.* Directions in Development. Washington, DC: World Bank.

Hanushek, E. A., S. Link, and L. Woessmann. 2011. "Does School Autonomy Make Sense Everywhere? Panel Estimate Form PISA." Working Paper 17591, National Bureau of Economic Research, Cambridge, MA.

Muralidharan, K., J. Das, A. Holla, and A. Mohpal. 2014. "The Fiscal Cost of Weak Governance: Evidence from Teacher Absence in India." Working Paper, National Bureau of Economic Research, Cambridge, MA.

CHAPTER 1

Who Are the Teachers?

Introduction

To understand teachers and teaching, this study has several interlinked parts. The first task is to understand Bihar's teachers, including their characteristics, family backgrounds, qualifications, training, and experience.

This section describes a teacher questionnaire administered in the schools selected for the study. Four hundred elementary schools were randomly selected from four districts of Bihar, comprising 100 schools each in East Champaran, Jamui, Purnea, and Rohtas. All teachers in these schools filled out questionnaires. The data from this round of responses are self-reported. A total of 2,252 teachers completed the questionnaire. Of the teachers included in this study, 2,119 were given the questionnaire during the first visit and 133 (those not interviewed in the first round) were covered during the second visit.

General Information about Teachers

Of the 2,252 teachers surveyed, a quarter taught in primary schools, and the rest taught in schools with combined sections of primary and upper primary classes (table 1.1).

All teachers in the selected schools were covered in the survey. About 22 percent were regular[1] teachers, and about 23 percent were *panchayat*[2] teachers (table 1.2). About half of the total comprised block level teachers (*prakhand shikshak*[3]).

The panchayat and block teachers are contractual teachers. They are appointed at the level of village panchayat for Classes (grades) I–V or block level for Classes (grades) I–VIII. From the distribution of teachers, it is clear that regular teachers are in a minority in the government schools. Close to three quarters of all teachers are on contract.

The distribution of teacher type varies by the type of school (table 1.3); primary schools have a much lower proportion of regular teachers (approximately 10 percent) compared with that of upper primary (about 26 percent). More than

Table 1.1 Teacher Distribution, by School Type

School type	n	%
Primary	559	24.82
Primary and upper primary	1,693	75.18
Total	**2,252**	**100**

Table 1.2 Type of Teachers

Type	Total	%
Head	56	2.5
Regular	501	22.3
Panchayat	512	22.7
Block	1,182	52.5
Total	**2,251**	**100**

Table 1.3 Type of Teacher, by School Type

	Primary		Upper primary	
Teacher type	n	%	n	%
Head	15	2.7	41	2.4
Regular	55	9.8	446	26.4
Panchayat	467	83.5	45	2.7
Block	22	3.9	1,160	68.6
Total	**559**	**100**	**1,692**	**100**

Table 1.4 Age Distribution, by Teacher Type
percent

Age (years)	Head	Regular	Panchayat	Block	Total
Younger than 20	3.6	2.0	28.4	28.3	21.8
20–29	14.3	11.6	55.2	54.1	43.9
30–39	23.2	39.6	13.9	15.7	20.8
40 and older	58.9	46.8	2.5	2.0	13.5
Total	**100**	**100**	**100**	**100**	**100**

80 percent of primary school teachers are panchayat, while upper primary schools have higher proportions of block teachers (about 69 percent).

Most teachers in Bihar's schools are young, with slightly less than half (about 44 percent) in the age range of 20–29 years (table 1.4).

The presence of larger proportions of young panchayat and block teachers contribute to this skew in the distribution of teachers in favor of youth. The age distributions demonstrate that head teachers and regular teachers on average are much

Table 1.5 Age Distribution of Teachers, by School Type
percent

Age (years)	Primary	Upper primary
Younger than 20	26.9	20.2
20–29	52.3	41.1
30–39	14.3	22.9
40 and older	6.5	15.8
Total	100	100

Table 1.6 Gender Distribution, by Age of Teacher

Age (years)	Male (%)	Female (%)	n
Younger than 20	42.2	57.8	491
20–29	61.1	38.9	988
30–39	65.5	34.5	467
40 and older	77.2	22.8	303
Total	60.1	39.9	2,249

Table 1.7 Teachers, by Caste

	General	Scheduled Caste	Scheduled Tribe	Other Backward Classes	Other	Total
Number	605	337	99	1,202	5	2,248
Percent	26.9	15	4.4	53.5	0.2	100

older than panchayat and block teachers. Comparing the age distribution of teachers by school type (table 1.5), we see that upper primary schools have a relatively large proportion of teachers who are more than 30 years old as compared with that of primary schools (about 38 percent and 21 percent, respectively).

Overall, close to 60 percent of all teachers surveyed were male. Female teachers were younger: about 58 percent of all teachers less than 20 years of age were female, and at higher age groups, the proportion of female teachers decreased (table 1.6).

Over half of all teachers surveyed were from the Other Backward Classes (OBC) category (table 1.7). In this study, caste information for children was not collected.

Teachers were asked additional questions, including their marital status, where their children attend school, where they live, and their daily commute time to school. Almost 90 percent of all teachers were married, and 84 percent had children of elementary school age. Of these, about 15 percent teachers reported sending their children to private schools; the rest attended government schools (table 1.8).

Around 30 percent of all teachers reported their village was the same as the school's village, and 32 percent stayed in the same village as the school. A little more than 45 percent lived in the same panchayat as the school in

Table 1.8 Teachers Whose Children Attend Government or Private Schools
percent

Children's age (years)	Government	Private	Total
5–10	84.1	15.9	100
11–14	85.0	15.0	100

Table 1.9 Teacher Types, by Location of Residence
percent

	Is the native village of the teacher the same village where the school is located?			Does the teacher stay in the same village as the school?			Does the teacher stay in the same panchayat as the school?		
	Yes	No	Total	Yes	No	Total	Yes	No	Total
Head teacher	16.1	83.9	100	16.1	83.9	100	21.4	78.6	100
Regular	12.2	87.8	100	18.4	81.6	100	17.8	82.2	100
Panchayat	27.1	72.9	100	29.9	70.1	100	52.2	47.9	100
Block	36.0	64.0	100	39.1	61.0	100	57.5	42.6	100
Total	**28.2**	**71.9**	**100**	**31.8**	**68.2**	**100**	**46.6**	**53.5**	**100**

Table 1.10 Teachers' Commute Time to School

Commute time to school	n	%
Less than or equal to 15 minutes	650	28.9
Less than 1 hour, more than 15 minutes	1,082	48.1
More than 1 hour	517	23.0
Total	**2,249**	**100**

which they worked. Also as one would expect, the panchayat and block teachers were more likely to stay in the same village or panchayat as the school compared with a head or a regular teacher (table 1.9). This information is important because it indicates that more than 50 percent of teachers (especially panchayat and block teachers) are local (in the same panchayat) and live quite close to the school in which they teach.

Close to 30 percent of the teachers had a travel time of 15 minutes or less, and most walked to school (40 percent). Only 23 percent of teachers had to travel more than an hour to the school in which they teach (table 1.10).

A majority of the teachers reported that they were not engaged in any other work activity other than teaching (66 percent). Of the remaining, farming was the most common work activity (approx. 64 percent) apart from teaching (table 1.11). Though farming was the main additional activity for male teachers, female teachers were involved in various other earning activities.

Turning to the employment history of the teachers in the study, table 1.12 shows that most regular teachers have been teachers for more than 15 years (the number since they were first appointed as teachers), while the panchayat and block teachers have come into the teaching profession as government school teachers only relatively recently. About 80 percent of panchayat and block teachers have been teachers for 10 years or less, which is not surprising given that the policy and practice of recruiting different kinds of teachers (other than regular teachers) is a relatively new phenomenon that goes back only about 10 to 12 years.

While head/regular teachers have a longer track record of teaching, on average they have spent fewer years teaching in their current school than is the case with block/panchayat teachers. Table 1.13 shows that most regular teachers had been teaching in the same school for less than five years (60 percent), while more than half of the block/panchayat teachers had been teaching in the same school for five to nine years.

Table 1.11 Teachers' Supplemental Work, by Type and Gender

Type	Total	Male (%)	Female (%)	Total (%)
Farming/dairy	483	69.7	32.5	63.6
Private	140	18.3	19.0	18.4
Politics/union work	125	15.3	22.2	16.4
Other earning work	65	4.7	27.8	8.6
Business/shop	21	1.9	7.1	2.8

Note: Teachers could report multiple options of work; therefore, the column total exceeds 100 percent.

Table 1.12 Years Teaching since Appointment, by Teacher Type
percent

Years since appointment	Head	Regular	Panchayat	Block	Total
Less than 5	10.9	31.8	34.4	28.7	30.3
5–9	14.6	12.6	52.1	58.3	45.6
10–14	14.6	11.2	11.6	12.9	12.2
More than 15	60.0	44.4	2.0	0.2	11.9
Total	100	100	100	100	100

Table 1.13 Years in Current School, by Teacher Type
percent

Years in current school	Head	Regular	Panchayat	Block	Total
Less than 5	51.8	60.2	37.6	31.5	39.8
5–9	35.7	26.6	51.9	56.7	48.4
More than 10	12.5	13.2	10.6	11.8	11.8
Total	100	100	100	100	100

Table 1.14 Transfers by Teacher Type
percent

Number of transfers	Head	Regular	Panchayat	Block	Total
None	19.6	31.9	92.4	92.8	77.3
1–2	41.1	43.1	6.4	6.8	15.7
3 or more	39.3	25.0	1.2	0.4	7.1
Total	**100**	**100**	**100**	**100**	**100**

The shorter time spent in a particular school by a head teacher or regular teacher can be attributed to frequent transfers (table 1.14). By contrast, by virtue of being local and more recently appointed, less than 10 percent of the block and panchayat teachers have been transferred.

Educational Qualifications and Training

We next look at the education and professional qualifications of teachers. The teachers were asked to mark their highest educational qualification out of the given five options. These options were below matric, matric,[4] intermediate,[5] graduate, and postgraduate.

The level of educational qualification reported by teachers is shown in figure 1.1. About 48 percent of all teachers are graduates or above (32 percent have graduate qualifications, and 16 percent have postgraduate qualifications).

Regular teachers are distributed relatively evenly across the qualification spectrum (figures 1.2 and 1.3). However, panchayat and block teachers are mostly either at the intermediate level (Class XII, or passed grade 12 with a high school certificate) or college/graduate level.

Teachers were also asked whether they have received any professional training. For this, teachers were asked to mark any one of the following options: no professional qualification, diploma, B.Ed., M.Ed., or other qualification related to the teaching profession. One-fourth of the teachers reported having some kind of professional qualification (apart from B.Ed., M.Ed., or diploma) while half said that they do not have any professional qualification (table 1.15).

After teachers are appointed, they are offered a variety of in-service trainings each year. These trainings range from one-day meetings to explain, for instance, filling formats, to longer capacity-building exercises. Many are intended to provide teachers with inputs and materials for improving content knowledge and delivery skills. Based on the data, we find that 63 percent did not receive any training during the year 2012–13 (table 1.16), although most teachers had attended one-day meetings or trainings.

Close to 64 percent teachers said that training helped in learning teaching methods and classroom activities (table 1.17). When asked what content they would choose for the next teacher training workshop, the largest proportion (66 percent) expressed a need for training in how to teach specific subjects and content areas.

Figure 1.1 Educational Qualification of Teachers
percent

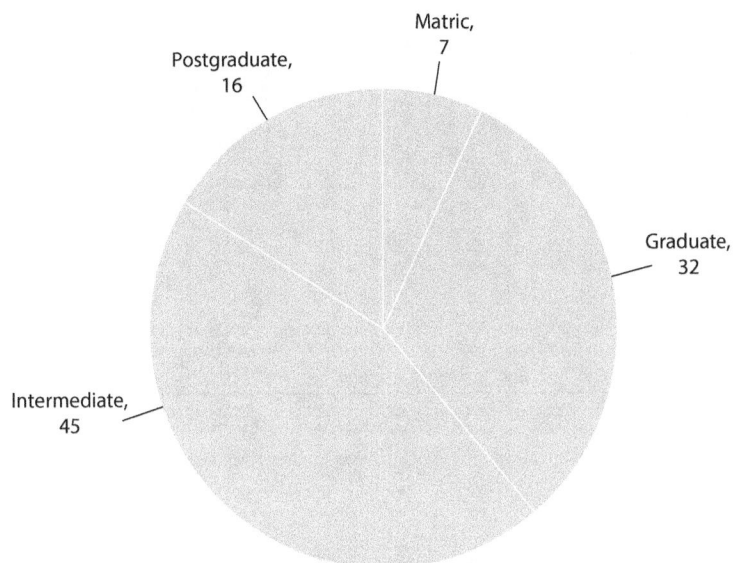

Note: Matric refers to those who have passed Class X (grade 10); intermediate refers to those who have passed Class XII (grade 12).

Figure 1.2 Educational Qualification, by Teacher Type
percent

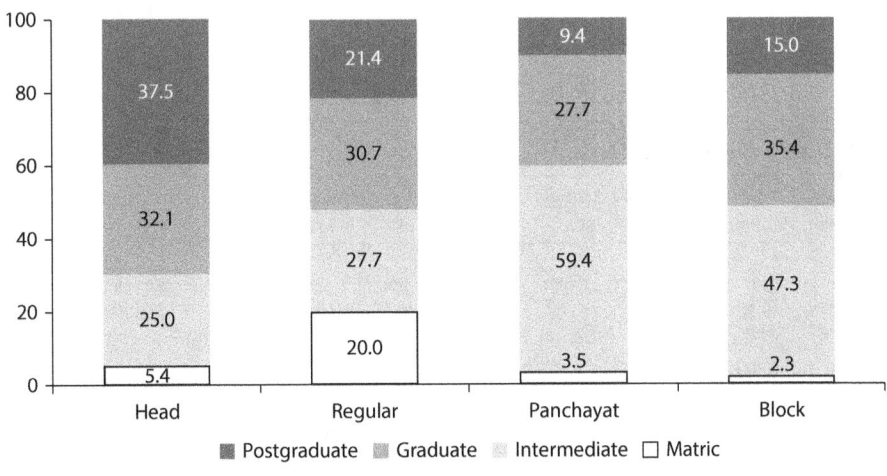

The questions asked and the data collected on teacher training in this study are clearly inadequate to reach any conclusions regarding teacher training. To track trainings and collect feedback from teachers, a set of preparatory tasks may be needed. For example, each year a number of trainings are planned (usually at the state level). It would be useful to analyze the objectives of each

Figure 1.3 Educational Qualification of Teachers, by Age
percent

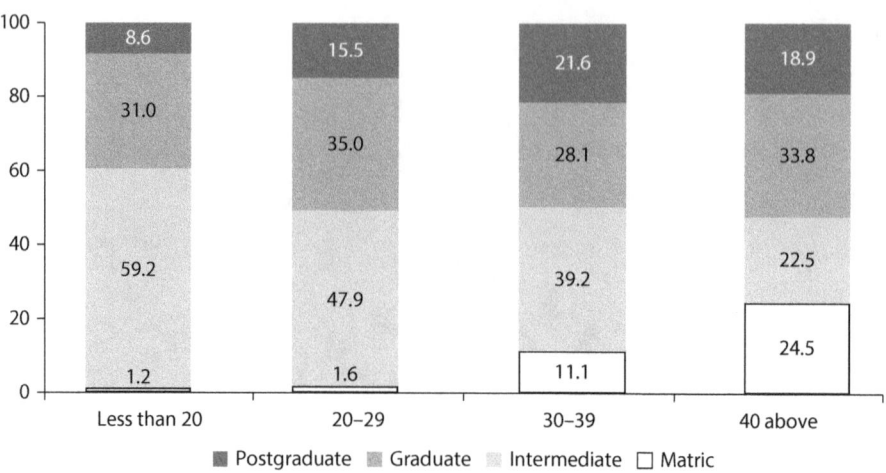

Table 1.15 Professional Qualifications of Teachers

Professional qualification	n	Percent
None	1,109	50.2
Diploma	313	14.2
B.Ed.	215	9.7
M.Ed.	16	0.7
Other	557	25.2
Total	2,210	100

Table 1.16 Days of Teacher Training, 2012–13

	How many days of training did you attend in the year 2012–13?		How many one-day training programs did you attend in the year 2012–13?	
	n	%	n	%
None	1,384	62.7	782	35.5
1–5	245	11.1	435	19.7
5–10	349	15.8	841	38.2
More than 10	228	10.3	146	6.6
Total	2,206	100	2,204	100

training and link them to a content and delivery pattern. A tracking system may be needed to check if all teachers for whom such training was intended indeed got the training. Feedback from teachers immediately after training and after some months would also elicit useful information and insights about the appropriateness of the training in actual teaching situations. Finally, the academic

Table 1.17 Training Feedback

	n	%
How has training helped teachers?		
Learned how to do some administrative work better (e.g., filling formats)	726	32.2
Learned some teaching methods or activities	1,442	64.0
Learned new things about policies, rules, or procedures in India or in Bihar	821	36.5
Learned some subject knowledge that was not known (e.g., fractions)	854	37.9
Did not learn anything that helps in the work	104	4.6
What content would you choose for the next teacher training workshop?		
Content knowledge in specific subject areas (e.g., in math or environmental studies [EVS])	1,053	46.76
How to teach specific subjects (e.g., language or science)	1,484	65.90
Multigrade teaching techniques	1,293	57.42
Classroom management techniques	1,176	52.22
How to interact with parents and the community	1,022	45.38
How to evaluate children's learning	1,191	52.89
Education policy in India and in Bihar	1,008	44.76
Other	174	7.73

monitoring work of cluster coordinators could also include observations of classroom practice to see if and how specific trainings relate to the work that teachers do on a regular basis.

Working in School: Activities and Attitudes

In trying to understand teachers in relation to their work in schools, we explored a few other features of what teachers report doing and thinking. Let us take a closer look at how teachers' work is organized in schools. Of all teachers surveyed, 30 percent in primary and 35 percent in upper primary schools said that they taught only one subject; the reference period was the day before the survey (table 1.18). At the other extreme, one-fifth of teachers in primary school taught four or more subjects. When asked about the classes (grades) taught on the day before the survey, most teachers reported teaching more than one class in both primary and upper primary school.

Finally, it is noteworthy that those teachers who reported teaching more classes on the previous working day were also teaching more subjects. Table 1.18 shows that the average number of subjects taught increases as the number of classes taught increases.

Time spent by teachers in school on various activities during a typical working week is shown in table 1.19. Teachers were asked to comment on a variety of activities and estimate the time involved in each of these per week. Teaching and preparing lessons were reported as being done quite often by a large majority of teachers (96 percent and 88 percent, respectively). This was followed by such activities as filling registers and preparing and serving midday meals (both approximately 70 percent).

Table 1.18 Distribution of Teachers by Classes (Grades) and Average Number of Subjects per Class

Number of classes taught	Teachers (%)	Number of subjects per class (average)
1	28.9	1.7
2 or 3	44.8	2.3
4 or 5	21.7	2.9
6, 7, or 8	4.6	3.8
Total	**100**	**2.3**

Note: Each teacher is expected to teach more than one grade—the table reflects the number of classes each teacher ends up teaching.

Table 1.19 Time Teachers Spent on Activities per Week
percent

Activities	Quite often[a]	Sometimes[b]	Never	Total
Teaching	96.3	3.2	0.5	100
Preparing lessons	87.6	10.9	1.5	100
Filling registers	69.5	17.0	13.4	100
CCE/other assessment activities	52.2	42.7	5.1	100
Preparing/serving midday meal	69.7	15.3	15.0	100
Extracurricular activities	58.1	35.0	6.9	100
Other administrative work	34.9	23.1	42.0	100

Note: CCE = Continuous Comprehensive Evaluation.
a. Quite often: every day, for more than 1 hour or less than 1 hour.
b. Sometimes: not every day but several hours per week or for a short time per week.

These data also suggest that time spent on preparing and serving the midday meal and other administrative work varies by type of teacher. Close to 90 percent of all head teachers work on preparing and serving the midday meal. A larger proportion of head teachers, followed by regular teachers, were found to work more often on other administrative work compared with panchayat or block teachers.

Overall, 20 percent teachers reported that they did not find any class difficult to teach (table 1.20). The majority of teachers find the highest grade (fifth for primary and eighth for upper primary) hardest to teach. Forty percent of panchayat teachers found the fifth class hardest to teach, and and around 33 percent of block teachers found the eighth class the hardest to teach. For regular teachers, the eighth class was most difficult to teach (about 34 percent).

Teachers were also asked whether they face any difficulties in teaching, and if they do, what help is available. About 21 percent teachers reported they faced no difficulty. Of those who faced difficulty, almost all reported receiving help (only 3 percent said nobody helps them). Most teachers used peer groups for guidance and also asked other teachers for help (table 1.21).

Teachers were asked whether and how often they had engaged in different class activities. For this, teachers were asked to report on the last time they did

Table 1.20 Hardest Class (Grade) to Teach, by Teacher Type
percent

Hardest class to teach	Head	Regular	Panchayat	Block	Total
None	15.4	22.4	19.0	18.8	19.6
Class I	11.5	9.8	17.7	9.6	11.4
Class II, III, or IV	7.7	12.0	18.4	11.5	13.0
Class V	30.8	6.0	39.9	6.9	14.2
Class VI or VII	7.7	16.1	2.9	20.4	15.5
Class VIII	26.9	33.8	2.2	32.8	26.3
Total	100	100	100	100	100

Table 1.21 Who Guides the Teachers?

Who guides?	Number	Percent
Head teacher	589	34.6
Other teacher/s	844	49.6
BRC/CRC	591	34.8
Other	125	7.4

Note: BRC = block resource center; CRC = cluster resource center.

Table 1.22 Time Spent on Teacher Activities
percent

Teacher activity	Quite often	Sometimes	Rarely or never	Total
Made a lesson plan?	82.3	11.4	6.3	100
Talked to a parent about the child's learning?	62.4	33.4	4.2	100
Used any TLM other than the textbook during a class?	78.6	14.0	7.3	100
Took out a book from the library?	61.6	17.6	20.7	100
Gave students homework?	94.9	3.3	1.8	100
Used the blackboard during a class?	94.0	2.2	3.7	100
Made children work in small groups during a class?	81.4	14.0	4.5	100
Were absent from school for half a day or more (including leave)?	21.3	26.6	52.0	100
Taught a group of two or three students together?	65.3	20.1	14.6	100
Helped to prepare or serve the midday meal?	77.6	12.0	10.4	100
Spent more than 1 hour in a day filling registers?	49.8	23.4	26.9	100
Visited the cluster or block resource center?	37.1	37.3	25.6	100
Asked somebody for help with teaching a topic?	30.4	30.7	38.9	100
Played a game/sports with students?	68.5	21.1	10.4	100
Did a class activity that was not mentioned in the textbook?	47.7	31.7	20.6	100

Note: TLM = teaching learning material.

a particular activity (table 1.22). Those who reported doing it the same day of the survey or in the last week were put in the category "quite often." Those who reported doing that activity during the last month or last three months were listed under "sometimes," while those who did the activity more than three months ago or never comprise the "rarely or never" category.

It is pertinent to remember that the data collected for this section of the report come from self-reported information. Most teachers reported that they gave students homework (95 percent). Almost all teachers (94 percent) used the blackboard during teaching, and 82 percent said they made lesson plans. A similar proportion reported that they made children work in small groups. Seventy-five percent of the head teachers said they visited the cluster or block center quite often. It is interesting that the data in the next chapter—based on classroom observations—give quite a different picture of teaching activities.

To explore teacher attitudes and perceptions, teachers were asked whether they agreed with certain statements. They were asked to mark their response on a scale from strongly agree to strongly disagree. These statements covered such topics as pedagogical practices and opinions about absenteeism. Ninety-six percent of teachers agreed with the statement, "I always make a lesson plan before teaching a class." Eighty-two percent of teachers said that they made a lesson plan quite often (table 1.23). Similarly, 88 percent of teachers agreed with the statement that they made their students work in groups in class. And 81 percent said that they do that quite often. About 85 percent teachers agreed with the statement that they knew the names of all their students.

Table 1.23 Teachers' Opinions
percent

Opinion	Agree[a]	Neither agree nor disagree	Disagree[b]	Total
Teachers who are often absent from school should be paid less.	62.9	17.3	19.8	100
All students are capable of learning mathematics.	74.3	9.9	15.8	100
I know the names of all the students I teach.	85.3	8.2	6.5	100
SC/ST students are less intelligent in comparison to other students.	29.7	11.6	58.8	100
If a child is absent for more than a week, I try to find out the reason.	97.4	1.1	1.5	100
If children don't learn well, it is the parents' responsibility.	58.0	16.5	25.5	100
Teachers whose students learn more should get higher salary.	40.7	20.7	38.6	100
I always make a lesson plan before teaching a class.	95.6	2.2	2.1	100
Most children in Class IV in my school know how to do subtraction.	86.4	6.8	6.9	100
The textbooks are too difficult for children.	35.3	14.3	50.4	100
Sometime I have difficulties in explaining math to my students.	60.8	6.9	32.4	100
I enjoy teaching and interacting with students.	96.5	1.4	2.1	100
To do well, students need private tuition as well as regular school.	42.5	12.0	45.4	100
When I have difficulty teaching a topic, I know how to get help.	88.6	4.0	7.3	100
The school does everything it can to help children learn well.	97.2	1.3	1.6	100
My objective as a teacher is to complete the syllabus.	87.5	2.9	9.6	100
I have met the parents of all of my students.	79.0	10.5	10.5	100
All the children in Class IV in this school can read fluently.	53.9	23.3	22.8	100
I often make children in my class work in groups.	88.3	5.8	5.8	100
Teaching was my first choice of jobs.	93.2	2.5	4.2	100

Note: SC = Scheduled Caste; ST = Scheduled Tribe.
a. Agree refers to the responses "agree" or "strongly agree."
b. Disagree refers to the responses "disagree" or "strongly disagree."

Close to 80 percent teachers agreed with the statement that they knew the parents of all their students, and 60 percent agreed that learning outcomes were the responsibility of the parent. Slightly more than 40 percent agree that students need private tuition to do well in school (table 1.23). About 63 percent teachers agreed with the statement that teachers who were often absent should be paid less; about 20 percent disagreed with the statement. However, only about 40 percent agreed with the statement that teachers whose students have better learning outcomes should be paid more; 39 percent disagreed.

Conclusion

This section provides an overview of a representative sample of elementary school teachers in Bihar. Understanding the teachers was the first step before diving deeper into what classrooms are like or how teachers teach. The data indicate that many are contract teachers (panchayat shikshak or prakhand/block shikshak) and are still quite young. They live in rural areas often less than an hour away from the school in which they teach. Their educational background is either at the intermediate or graduate levels, but most do not have professional qualification or certifications in teaching or education.

Notes

1. Regular teachers are those who are hired by the Bihar Public Service Commission on a full pay as compared with teachers on a contractual basis who are hired by the panchayats.
2. Panchayat is the smallest unit of local government—usually a group of villages.
3. Prakhand is a block, or unit, in the subdistrict level administrative structure of a district.
4. Matric refers to those who have passed Class X (grade 10).
5. Intermediate refers to those who have passed Class XII (grade 12).

CHAPTER 2

What Are Classrooms Like?

Introduction

In this study of teachers and teaching in Bihar, a variety of methods was used to gain a better understanding of who the teachers are and what they do in the classroom. Self-reported data from teachers were analyzed to get a sense of their background, their educational qualifications and training experiences, and their tenure as a teacher (chapter 1). Questionnaires were used to get details of teacher activities and attitudes, also discussed in chapter 1.

Moving beyond self-reported information from teachers to actual classroom observations is a critical step of any study that focuses on teaching. Clearly, spending time observing classrooms provides an important perspective on teaching. However, a single visit to observe classrooms and schools is not sufficient. The conditions prevailing in a school can change on a day-to-day basis depending on who is present, what is to be done on that day, and what is happening in the village. School environments also change during the year. Rural schools face disruptions as a result of weather-based seasonal changes, agricultural activities, festivals, the marriage season, and activities and changes in the school calendar. Hence, visiting schools and classrooms periodically, or at least several times a year, is useful. Repeat visits allow us to see if the activities or organizational patterns that we observe are of a permanent nature or if they are different each time.

The fieldwork for this study of teachers and teaching was carried out between September 2013 and July 2014. This time period straddles two school years: 2013–14 and 2014–15. During this period, there were three visits to the sampled schools. The first visit was between the middle of September and end of October 2013. The second visit was in December of 2013. The last visit was in July 2014, after schools reopened following the summer break.

For the classroom observations, we focused on two classes—Class IV and Class VI. To keep consistency and comparability between schools and over time, we observed only language and math classes.[1] Teaching in other subjects was not observed. Focus on these two subjects also made it easier to relate the classroom observation data to the information from the teacher questionnaire, where only language and math questions had been covered.

Given that this study was a large-scale, primarily quantitative exercise, spanning 400 schools and more than 600 classrooms that were visited three times each, classroom observations were concentrated on a set of indicators that are the core of teaching activities but relatively easy to observe. The observation indicators were also designed for potential future use, particularly by those who visit schools routinely to support and monitor teaching and learning interactions in classrooms. The observation indicators, or checklist, focused on two broad domains: the classroom organization and environment and teaching activities.

For classroom organization, we looked at such features as which classes, or grades, were sitting together, the physical location of the class, the physical organization of the class (groups or rows), the basic infrastructure in the class, and the use of timetables.

For teaching activities, we focused on basic teaching methods (what the teacher was doing), the interaction between teachers and children (who talked to whom), and student activities (what students were doing). The observer spent a continuous period of 30 minutes in the classroom observed. Almost all questions were marked either *yes* or *no*.

In the first visit, Class IV and Class VI classes were visited in all schools—primary and upper primary. But because of time constraints in visits 2 and 3, observers visited Class IV and Class VI classrooms in only the upper primary schools. Almost all upper primary government schools in Bihar have classes from Class I and Class VIII. Therefore, the data reported in the rest of this section refer only to the subset of classes for which we have information for all three visits (i.e., selected grades in the upper primary schools). Thus, for purposes of this discussion, we have about 200 classes for each grade (1,277 class visits)[2] that have been visited three times during the course of the study (table 2.1).

Classroom Organization and Classroom Environment

Where Are Classes Held?

The observation tool starts with recording the physical location of the class to be observed. Was the class in a classroom? In the verandah? Outdoors? The data indicate that close to 90 percent of all classes were conducted indoors in classrooms (table 2.2). The proportion of children sitting outdoors in the second visit was reportedly due to the weather conditions. In December, it is common to see classes held outdoors in the sunshine even if the school has an adequate number

Table 2.1 Total Number of Classroom Visits, 2013–14

Month of visit	Class IV	Class VI
Visit 1: Sept.–Oct. 2013	213	212
Visit 2: Dec. 2013	214	212
Visit 3: July 2014	214	212
Total	641	636

Table 2.2 Location of Observed Classes, Upper Primary Schools

Visit	Class IV Total visited	Class location (%)			Class VI Total visited	Class location (%)		
		Classroom	Verandah	Outdoors		Classroom	Verandah	Outdoors
Visit 1: Sept.–Oct. 2013	211	93.8	4.3	1.9	209	97.1	1.9	1.0
Visit 2: Dec. 2013	205	77.6	4.9	17.6	209	88.5	1.0	10.5
Visit 3: July 2014	211	93.4	4.3	2.4	210	95.2	3.3	1.4
Average		88.3	4.5	7.3	Average	93.6	2.1	4.3

Table 2.3 Incidence of Multigrade Classes, Class IV

Visit	One grade in classroom		Two grades in classroom		More than two grades in classroom		Total grades observed	
	n	%	n	%	n	%	n	%
Visit 1: Sept.–Oct. 2013	93	44.1	86	40.8	32	15.2	211	100
Visit 2: Dec. 2013	97	47.3	76	37.1	32	15.6	205	100
Visit 3: July 2014	85	40.3	99	46.9	27	12.8	211	100
Average	91.7	43.9	87	41.6	30.3	14.5	209	100
Total classes visited	275		261		91		627	

of classrooms. Overall, across the three visits, for both grades that were studied and at least for the upper primary schools, 9 times out of 10, the class was held in a classroom.

How Common Is It for Different Grades to Be Taught Together?

For a long time and until very recently, Bihar had been plagued with acute shortages of teachers and space. Hence, it used to be very common to see multigrade arrangements in primary and upper primary schools. For example, a study conducted in 2007–08 visited a sample of 160 schools across Bihar four times during the school year (Kingdon and Banerji 2009). That study, as with the current one, had repeated unannounced visits to schools making it possible to observe the dynamic nature of school functioning. The 2007–08 study found only 7 percent cases where in each visit the class being observed was the only grade being taught.

With large numbers of teachers entering the education system in the last ten years and with an expansion in infrastructure, the incidence of multigrade groupings has declined considerably. Tables 2.3 (Class IV) and 2.4 (Class VI) show the current situation in the upper primary schools in the four districts selected for the study.

The data suggest that multigrade groupings are more common in primary grades (such as Class IV) as compared with grades at the upper primary level (such as Class VI) even in the same school. Close to 60 percent of all Class VI classes observed were single grade, while only 44 percent or so of Class IV classes

Table 2.4 Incidence of Multigrade Classes in Observed Schools in Bihar, Class VI

	One grade in classroom		Two grades in classroom		More than two grades in classroom		Total grades observed	
	No.	%	No.	%	No.	%	No.	%
Visit 1: Sept.–Oct. 2013	132	63.2	41	19.6	36	17.2	209	100
Visit 2: Dec. 2013	125	59.8	41	19.6	43	20.6	209	100
Visit 3: July 2014	122	58.1	49	23.3	39	18.6	210	100
Average	126.3	60.4	43.7	20.8	39.3	18.8	209.3	100
Total classes visited	**379**		**131**		**118**		**628**	

Table 2.5 Multigrade Classrooms for Class IV by School Type, Visit 1
percent

School type	One grade in classroom	Two grades in classroom	More than two grades in classroom	Total
Primary	14.0	42.5	43.6	100
Upper primary	44.1	40.8	15.2	100

sat by themselves (table 2.4). The incidence of two grades sitting together in Class IV at 41.6 percent is almost double of that seen in Class VI (20.8 percent). More than two grades sitting together is a far less likely option (well below 20 percent for both grades).

In visit 1, Class IV classrooms were observed in primary schools and in the schools that also had primary and upper primary sections. Because of time constraints, from visit 2 onward, classroom observations were done only in the two selected grades in the upper primary schools. But data from the first visit allow us to get a snapshot of what Class IV is like in both types of schools. The visit 1 data show a major difference between primary and upper primary schools in terms of multigrade classrooms (table 2.5). A large proportion of Class IV classes (43.6 percent) in primary schools comprised more than two grades as compared with upper primary schools (15.2 percent).

In each visit we observed that there were some schools where Class IV and Class VI children were sitting by themselves; there was no other grade clubbed or grouped with them for teaching purposes. But is this a permanent feature of this school? Do these classes in these schools always follow this pattern? The incidence of monograde classrooms across all three visits is shown in table 2.6. As compared with the previous average of approximately 44 percent in Class IV and 60 percent in Class VI, the percentage of monograde classes in all three visits falls to about 30 percent and about 45 percent, respectively.

While looking at table 2.6, it is worth remembering that the situation with Class IV in schools that have primary sections may be only considerably worse. In the 2007–08 study of primary schools, the percentage of schools that had monograde classrooms across all four visits was about 7 percent. Looking at the data from visit 1, it is possible to assume that the same figure for this study may

Table 2.6 Monograde in All Three Visits, Upper Primary Schools

	Total number in all three visits	Monograde in all three visits	
		No.	%
Class IV	201	61	30.3
Class VI	205	93	45.4

Table 2.7 Multigrade Classes by Number of Teachers in the School, Class IV

No. of teachers in school	% of schools	One grade in classroom	Two grades in classroom	More than two grades in classroom	Total grades observed (%)
≤6	32.1	12.82	52.82	34.36	100
7–10	43.0	46.67	45.19	8.15	100
More than 10	24.9	76.58	22.15	1.27	100
Total	100.0	43.66	41.73	14.61	100

Table 2.8 Multigrade Classes by Number of Teachers in the School, Class VI

No. of teachers in school	% of schools	One grade in classroom	Two grades in classroom	More than two grades in classroom	Total grades observed (%)
≤6	32.1	26.67	30.77	42.56	100
7–10	43.0	66.54	22.06	11.4	100
More than 10	24.9	91.08	7.01	1.91	100
Total	100.0	60.26	20.99	18.75	100

have gone up, but it is still likely to be well below 14 percent. Does this mean that despite the massive recruitment of teachers in the last few years, the huge expansion of schools has not improved classroom organization or grouping substantially in the schools where there are only primary sections? Is this one of the features of "overuniversalization" or of creating schools in every habitation?

How Does the Incidence of Multigrade Classes Vary by the Number of Teachers Available in a School?

As one would expect, the higher the availability of teachers in a school, the lower the likelihood of multigrade classrooms. The probability of a grade (either Class IV or Class VI) being the only grade in the classroom is very low if there are six or less teachers in a school. However, this probability jumps up if there are seven or more teachers appointed in a school.

Table 2.7 shows that when there are more than 10 teachers in an upper primary school, more than 75 percent of Class IV classes are sitting by themselves. For Class VI (table 2.8), the incidence of single-grade classrooms is even higher, at 91 percent.

Despite improvements over time in the availability of teachers at the school level, it is still worth noting that significantly large proportions of Class IV and

Class VI classes are taught with other grades in the same classroom. With teachers not adequately equipped to deal with multigrade contexts, this is a major challenge for Bihar. Depending on the academic monitoring and support mechanisms that are in place, figuring out how to organize grade groupings effectively and systematically is an important task that needs to be done school by school. If two or more grades have to be grouped together, then which two are the best to merge has to be decided by taking the ground realities of each school into account. If a district has such issues, then a standardized way to group children may help the district to prepare the teachers better for these situations in their in-service training periods.

Is There Enough Space for Teachers and Students? Are There Adequate Materials for Teaching?

The checklist used for observing classroom facilities was broadly divided into whether there was space for children to sit or for teachers to walk up to every child, whether there were blackboards and chalk for use, and if there was any educational material other than textbooks visible in the room.

Looking at the classroom infrastructure data collected from schools across all three visits combined (table 2.9), it seems that classrooms did have space for students and teachers, and usually had usable and visible blackboards in all three visits. However, classrooms lacked the presence of Teaching Learning Material (TLM) (other than textbooks) and displays of children's work. Hardly any classrooms had either of these two kinds of materials in all three visits.

In terms of seating arrangement, children sat individually in rows (rather than in a circle or in small groups) in more than 95 percent of all classrooms on all visits. This is a traditional classroom seating pattern and seems to be widespread in Bihar.

Given that classroom conditions are quite different in the two kinds of schools, we now look more closely at the data from visit 1, which allows a comparison of Class IV classes between primary schools and upper primary schools.

Table 2.9 Classroom Infrastructure, Total of Three Visits
percent

	Class IV	Class VI
There is space for all children present to sit comfortably.	79.1	84.9
There is space for the teacher to walk up to every child.	73.1	80.5
All children are sitting on chairs.	20.4	37.6
All children are sitting on mats or tat pattis.[a]	52.2	31.7
There is a blackboard that is easy to write on.	66.7	79.0
The children in the back can easily see the writing on the blackboard.	65.2	77.1
There is chalk in the classroom.	58.7	59.5
There is TLM (other than textbooks) visible in the classroom.	0.5	0.5
Children's creative work is displayed on the walls.	0.0	1.0

Note: TLM = teaching learning material.
a. Floor mats used for children to sit on.

As shown in table 2.10, for most indicators only marginal differences were observed between primary and upper primary schools. Arrangements for children's seating showed the biggest difference, with far more Class IV children in upper primary schools sitting on chairs as opposed to those in primary schools, who were more often sitting on tat pattis. In addition, TLM and children's creative work were observed slightly more often in Class IV classrooms located in primary schools as compared with in upper primary schools.

What about Timetables?

Almost all schools (more than 90 percent) and all observed classes reported having a timetable, but there was a great deal of variation in where the timetable could be found (table 2.11). For about one-fourth of all schools, the timetable was displayed on the wall of the observed classroom. In another 30 percent of cases, the timetable could be seen on the wall elsewhere in the school but not in the classroom being observed. In slightly less than 50 percent of the observations, the timetable was neither displayed in the classroom nor elsewhere in the school. In these cases, either the teacher or the headmaster/mistress showed the observer the timetable.

Table 2.10 Classroom Infrastructure by School Type, Visit 1, Class IV
percent

	Primary	Upper primary
There is space for all children present to sit comfortably.	86.0	86.8
There is space for the teacher to walk up to every child.	84.9	84.0
All children are sitting on chairs.	16.1	34.6
All children are sitting on *tat pattis*.	79.0	63.2
There is a blackboard that is easy to write on.	76.3	89.6
The children in the back can easily see the writing on the blackboard.	96.5	98.4
There is TLM (other than textbooks) visible in the classroom.	14.0	10.4
Children's creative work is displayed on the walls.	13.4	9.0

Note: TLM = teaching learning material.

Table 2.11 Timetable Indicators
percent

Classes where timetable related indicators are visible[a]	Class IV	Class VI
Is there a timetable in the school?	90.4	90.8
If there is a timetable, where was it visible?		
Displayed in the wall in the classroom	22.9	24.4
Displayed on the wall somewhere in the school not in the classroom	30.7	30.0
With the headmaster, not displayed anywhere	33.2	32.5
With the teacher, not displayed anywhere	13.2	13.2

a. Timetable indicator followed very similar pattern across visits. The data are an average across all visits for each class. Wherever the timetable was available, it was being followed.

The current situation as observed in this study is quite different from the research carried out in 2007–08, where only 25 percent of schools had class-specific timetables and, among those that did, only 35 percent were found following the timetable. (The 2007–08 study focused on primary grades only.)

Overall, a quick glance at how classrooms were organized seems to suggest that most classes were in rooms. There was enough space for the children to sit comfortably and for the teacher to move around. Children were mostly sitting on chairs or more likely on mats. The seating arrangement was almost always in rows, with individual children sitting one behind the other, regardless of what they were sitting on. Multigrade grouping, at least in terms of two grades sitting together, is still prevalent—although more so in primary grades than in upper primary classes. But close to half of all classes observed (44 percent for Class IV and 60 percent for Class VI) had only one grade sitting alone. And there was a timetable for the classes, whether the actual timetable was visible or not. Since the two grades being observed were in the same school, it was not surprising to find similar patterns of classroom organization across grades.

Classroom and Teaching Activities

Although surveyors were told to observe either math or language classes, once the data were analyzed it became clear that almost all the classroom observations were of language classes (95 percent of the classroom observations for both grades are for language).

Classroom observation had three parts: activities that the teachers were doing and activities that most students were doing in the same period of 30 minutes. Third, it also attempted to look at visible and broad ways in which teacher attitudes toward students could be observed.

How Do Teachers Teach?

From simply enumerating how many activities a teacher did during a 30-minute period (table 2.12), it appears as though there is a lot of variation. However, most of these activities were being done by the teacher and were related to directly transmitting textbook content to children—reading aloud, writing textbook content on the blackboard, and asking children to write that in their notebooks.

Observations from more than 400 classrooms suggest that most of the time, most teachers, regardless of grade level, use traditional teaching methods. Much of the activity during the class is squarely centered on the textbook and is largely teacher-driven. For example, most of the teachers were observed reading from the textbook (89 percent) and asking oral questions to students from the textbook (67 percent) or asking students to recite (49 percent). Fifty-seven percent of teachers were observed writing on the blackboard—usually content from the textbook—and in 44 percent of the classes students were asked to write (in their notebooks or slates). In less than one-fifth of classrooms did we see teachers ask students to come to the blackboard and write anything. It was also rare to see

Table 2.12 Variation in Teaching Activities
percent

Teaching activities[a]	Teachers doing variety of activities in class (30 min. observation period)	
	Class IV	Class VI
Doing fewer than 3 activities	27.4	22.6
Doing 3 or 4 activities	40.4	42.0
Doing 5 or more activities	32.2	35.5
Total	100	100

a. Patterns of activities were quite similar across visits. Data in this table are based on an average across three visits.

teachers ask children to work in groups or use any material other than textbooks or do any activity unrelated to textbooks.

Summarizing data from the observation of student activities, we see the mirror image of what teachers do in the classroom. In most classes, students were observed to be reading. Much of the reading activity was reading from the textbook (74 percent). In hardly any classrooms did we see children reading anything other than textbooks (5 percent).

Compared with reading (which we saw in 75 percent of the observed classes), it was relatively less common to see students writing (50 percent of observed classes). But even when children were seen writing, it was mostly copying from the blackboard (in 43 percent of classes) or taking dictation (24 percent). In hardly any classrooms did we observe students doing any other kind of writing activity (11 percent). Overall, we did not see much student activity regarding anything other than the textbook or based on anything that was not directed by teachers.

Are Teachers' Own Reports about Their Activities Very Different from What They Are Observed to be Doing in the Classroom?

The answer is yes. As described in chapter 1, all teachers in the sampled schools were asked to fill out a questionnaire. In this survey format, among other information, they were asked about their different activities.[3] Here are some examples of what teachers say they do, which are very different from what they were actually observed doing.

- 78.6 percent of teachers reported that they often use educational materials other than textbooks during a class. However, classroom observations do not suggest that this is the case. In less than 17 percent of classrooms was any material other than textbooks visible.
- 81.4 percent of teachers report that they often make children work in small groups. However, this was rarely observed in the classrooms that were visited on three separate occasions.
- At least half of all teachers surveyed said that they often did activities that were not mentioned in the textbook. But the classroom visits indicated that teachers rarely depart from the textbook in any way.

Understanding why teachers' responses are different from their practice is a matter of interpretation. It is possible that teachers know what elements of good teaching are (like group work, assigning tasks to students to do on their own, contextualizing tasks, or using a variety of materials) but are unable to do it in their classroom. A clear implication of this discrepancy is that when teachers are being trained (in-service or preservice) a great deal of attention has to be paid to demonstrate and help teachers to translate theoretical concepts into practice. Knowing about "child-centered" pedagogy is not helpful unless the teachers are actually able to do it.[4]

Teacher-Student Interaction

What Can We Say about How Teachers Relate to Students from Observing Their Interactions?

In this study, the observation schedule attempted to go beyond the basic characteristics of what teachers and students were doing and look for direct and measureable indicators for how the teacher–student interaction could be characterized.

Observers were asked to record a few basic kinds of interactions between teachers and students. Here are some examples of indicators:

- Did the teacher approach at least three individual students in the middle or back of the class?
- Did the teacher refer to at least three students by name during teaching?
- Did the teacher smile, laugh, or joke with the students at all during the class?
- Did the teacher use any local information to make the lesson more relevant to the students?

These kinds of practices were coded as "positive attitude to students." Among "negative" practices, we included the following:

- Did you see the teacher giving corporal punishment to students?
- Did you see the teacher carrying a cane or stick in the classroom?
- Did you hear the teacher using negative language with children?

We also used two simple indicators for engagement in teaching:

- Did you see the teacher doing any nonteaching work during the class?
- Did you observe the teacher leaving the classroom before the class was over?

At least during the observation time, hardly any teachers displayed any negative behavior. In less than 4 percent of the cases did the observers see any teachers administering corporal punishment, carrying a cane or stick, or using negative or derogatory language. Also, while the observations were going on, hardly any teachers were seen doing any nonteaching work (2.5 percent) or leaving the classroom before the class was over (8.2 percent).

Table 2.13 Teacher–Student Interactions: Positive Activities
percent

Observed activities[a]	Low (0 or 1 positive activities)	Medium (2 positive activities)	High (3 or 4 positive activities)	Total
Class IV	48.1	35.0	16.9	100
Class VI	43.2	37.5	19.2	100

a. These data are averaged over classroom observations across three visits.

About 63 percent of teachers in the observed classrooms were interacting with students sitting toward the middle or back of the class. In almost as many classes, we saw teachers addressing individual students by name. But it was far less common to see teachers smiling or joking with the students (11 percent). Of course, this can easily be attributed to the presence of the observer in the classroom.

Based on table 2.13, we can see that in at least half of all observed classrooms, teachers did two or more positive activities that showed their positive attitude to their students.

Conclusion

The three visits to the sampled schools and the classroom observations in the sampled grades are helpful in providing a glimpse of basic teaching practices in Bihar's elementary schools. Overall, the data show that most of the teaching happens in a fairly traditional way. Children sit in rows and work individually. There is hardly any group work. The textbook is at the center of the class interactions. Teachers transmit textbook content mainly by reading and writing on the board. There is not much activity done by teachers or students that does not involve the textbook. There was no corporal punishment during the observation period.

As more investment is done in Bihar in teacher training and professional development over the next few years, the substance of classroom interactions may change. Interactive practices in teaching, active participation of students, group work, and reliance on a greater variety of educational materials may all look different if such classroom observations are done some years from now. However, to move away from ingrained and traditional teaching practices, teacher training may need to have "learning by doing" components, in which different classroom interactions are demonstrated and modeled and teachers are asked to practice. Ongoing and effective mechanisms of field-based support will need to be developed to change teaching habits and traditions.

Notes

1. Once the classroom observation data were analyzed, it became clear that a majority of the classrooms observed were Hindi classes.
2. Class visits: 641 + 636 = 1,277.

3. Keep in mind that the teachers observed in the classroom are a subset of all teachers who filled out the teacher questionnaire.
4. Such discrepancies have been observed in previous studies as well. See the classroom observation chapter in the "Inside Primary Schools" study (http://www.asercentre.org/p /62.html).

Reference

Kingdon, Geeta, and Rukmini Banerji. 2009. "Addressing School Quality: Some Policy Pointers from Rural North India." Policy Brief 5 (September), Research Consortium on Educational Outcomes and Poverty, Cambridge, UK.

CHAPTER 3

Teacher Assessments

Introduction

An effective teacher has many characteristics. Classroom observations can highlight the visible dimensions of teaching practice, but there are many other attributes that are less immediately visible. Subject matter knowledge, ability to communicate, classroom management, and empathy toward students are all essential ingredients for teaching well.

It is worth remembering that the study covers 400 schools in Bihar and more than 2,200 elementary school teachers. Despite this scale, we still wanted to investigate teachers' subject matter knowledge, their ability to communicate to children, and their ability to be flexible to children's needs. Based on past empirical work on this topic and on field experience in government school settings in Bihar and other states, a framework was developed. This framework is anchored to the reality of our classrooms and on activities that could substantially help to improve the core of teaching in Indian schools. The focus is on how teachers teach basic skills in language and math in primary grades. Three broad categories of practices were selected for closer investigation using a pen and paper, written format:[1]

> Correcting children's work and inferring what children know or don't know from children's work: A substantial part of teachers' time both inside and outside the classroom is spent on correcting children's work. What exactly do teachers do when they correct? Do they simply correct and provide the right answer? Do teachers use children's work as a source of information for teaching? A set of questions were included in the teacher assessment questionnaire. These items are based on samples of children's work in language and arithmetic and used to explore teacher practice around corrections. The objective was to bring the reality of the classrooms into this exercise.

> Explaining content using language and methods that could be easily understood by children: It is quite common in India to find that the grade-level textbook content and language are too difficult for children. One of the challenges of teaching is to develop a bridge between what the child is supposed to know and what the child

currently knows. Thus, being able to explain concepts and content in an accessible and systematic way is an important skill for teachers to have and to use. The set of tasks was included in the teacher assessment questionnaire to see whether teachers were able to bridge this gap. These tasks included asking teachers to summarize a given text, requesting that they use simple language to explain difficult words, and having them write step-by-step solutions to given math problems.

Developing new questions based on content that was given to them: Although textbooks or other materials are available to teachers and students, it is expected that teachers will go beyond what is presented in textbooks. This is needed for many reasons, and at least two are explored in this study. First: is the teacher able to make contextually relevant questions for his or her children? The relevance could be with respect to language (for example, is it local or accessible?) or to local contexts and realities that are linked to the level of children. Second: is the teacher able to go beyond the boundaries of what is presented in the textbook and link curricular content to the everyday life of students?[2]

In the language and math sections that follow, more details will be discussed for each of these domains and how they are operationalized for use in the teacher questionnaire.

Four hundred government schools were covered in this study—100 schools from each of the four districts (Purnia, in the northeastern part of the state bordering West Bengal; East Champaran, in the northwest near Uttar Pradesh; Jamui, in the southeast; and Rohtas, in the southwest). In each district, half of the schools in the study are primary schools, and the rest of the schools have primary and upper primary sections. We received 2,206 teacher questionnaires from the government school teachers in these districts. The grading of the teacher survey questionnaire was done by a team selected by the Bihar government's State Council of Educational Research and Training (SCERT), assisted by staff from the ASER Centre. Decisions on the grading rubrics and other criteria were jointly developed by this team.

The questionnaire on teaching and assessment was administered to all teachers in the sampled schools. All teachers in sampled schools (primary and upper primary sections) were asked to participate in the math and language assessments. The assessment was administered to a group of teachers seated in a classroom at the same time. Two samples were provided for each subject. Teachers sitting adjacent to each other were given different samples. The total time given to complete both subjects was three hours. The teachers were supposed to write their answers in the space given in the question paper. Surveyors gave the instructions only at the start of the exercise. They did not resolve any questions or doubts during the test. The surveyors were told not to provide any additional instructions or examples that were not written in the questionnaire. The surveyors ensured that teachers did not consult with each other during the assessment. Every teacher was supposed to work on his or her answer sheet and hand it in. Thus the data in this section are based on teachers' self-reported responses collected in a pen and paper format.

Teacher Questionnaire and Teacher Assessment: Math

The framework for the assessment of teaching math is anchored around the broad domains[3] presented in table 3.1.

In the following sections, we discuss each of these items in some detail, laying out the findings, interpretations, and implications for action. For each item and wherever possible, we describe each task, outline how grading was done, provide examples of teachers' work, and summarize teachers' performance.

Given the constraints of time, only a limited set of questions could be asked that explored the teaching of math.[4] Despite the limited set of questions that could be used, it is possible that the tasks in this study could provide valuable inputs into future work.

Correcting Children's Mistakes

If you talk to an elementary school teacher in India in general about challenges in teaching, sooner or later the teacher will bring up the issue of how much of his or her time goes into correcting children's written work and how time-consuming it is to keep up with corrections, especially in large classes. If corrections are indeed a major activity, then it is worth understanding the different dimensions of how teachers cope with them.

In the math assessment of this study, we focused on three aspects of corrections.

- Can the teacher correctly identify the mistakes the child is making?
- Can the teacher show how to get to the correct answer?
- What can the teacher say about what a child knows or doesn't know after looking at his or her written work?

To explore these three aspects we used two tasks: one was a division problem and the other a two-digit addition problem. Both these examples of children's work are based on very common mistakes that children make in computations.

Correcting Division

Children often have difficulty solving long division problems. We chose this as an example of children's work. The teacher was shown how three different

Table 3.1 Framework for Mathematics Assessment

Serial number	Domain	Description of items and tasks
1	Understanding children's mistakes	These items investigate the ability of teachers to identify and correct mistakes commonly made by children.
2	Explaining processes and solving problems[a]	These items assess the teacher's ability to apply and solve problems and explain the method (arithmetic, mensuration, data interpretation, percentage computations, and unitary method).
3	Developing questions and problems	These items explore the teacher's ability to create appropriate questions for children on given topics.

a. This is a combination of content knowledge and ability to explain.

students solved a 3-digit by 1-digit, long division problem. The teacher was then asked to identify which child had done the problem correctly. And as the logical next step, the teacher was asked to show step by step how to solve the problem[5] (figure 3.1).

Table 3.2 shows that close to 80 percent of all teachers were able to correctly identify which child did the division problem correctly. However 16 percent could not identify the correct response, and 4 percent did not attempt this question.

Showing All Computational Steps Correctly as Part of Correction

In the second part of the question, an example was shown depicting all the steps needed to explain clearly the processes involved in solving a division problem

Figure 3.1 Sample Response: Can Teachers Do Division with All the Steps?

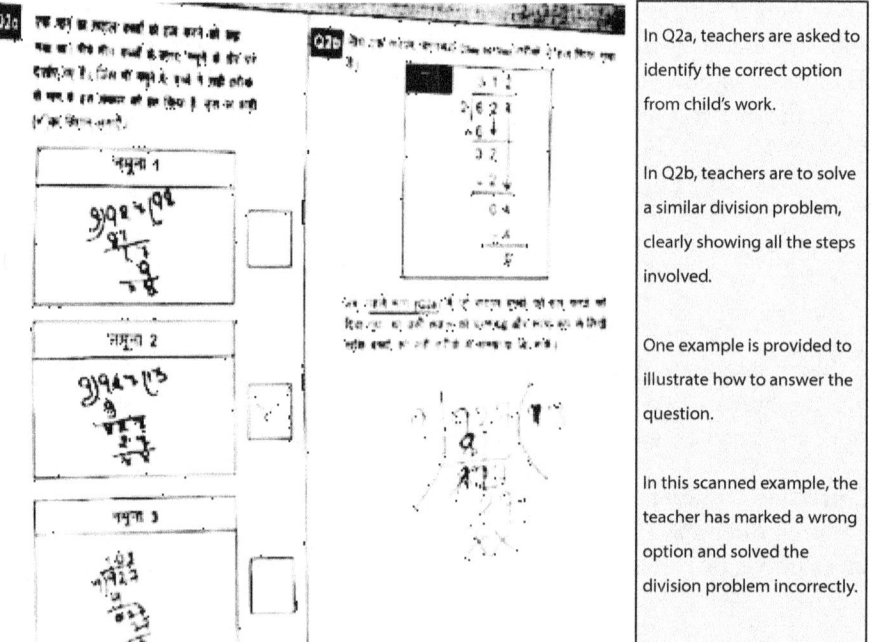

In Q2a, teachers are asked to identify the correct option from child's work.

In Q2b, teachers are to solve a similar division problem, clearly showing all the steps involved.

One example is provided to illustrate how to answer the question.

In this scanned example, the teacher has marked a wrong option and solved the division problem incorrectly.

Table 3.2 Teachers' Ability to Identify Children's Mistakes

Ability	percent
Correctly identified which child had completed the problem correctly	79.8
Could not identify correctly which child had completed the problem correctly	16.0
No response	4.2
Total	100

(3 digit by 1 digit). Textbooks and teacher guides also have such examples. As a very common task and classroom practice, the teacher writes down the correct steps on the blackboard for the children to see. For this task, the teachers had to write down the correct process and steps for solving the problem. It was expected that teachers would write all the required steps, especially since an example was given.

To grade whether the teacher was able to explain all the steps correctly we used three criteria:

- Was the teacher able to solve the division task correctly? (Were the quotient and the remainder correct?)
- Did the teacher show all necessary steps? (Three steps needed to be shown.)
- In the steps shown, were all elements present? (For example, was the minus sign included in the division problem?)

As in the case of identifying which child had done the question correctly, here, too, a very large percentage of teachers could solve the division problem correctly (table 3.3). Being able to understand and solve numerical division problems is a key part of the primary school math curriculum and a basic competency that needs to be in place before moving to higher skills. This type of question may be a good proxy for a whole host of capabilities related to knowing and teaching basic mathematical operations.

The data show that close to 80 percent of all teachers knew the right answer, so it can be assumed that content or subject matter knowledge is not the problem.[6] However, in explaining the steps of how to solve a math problem, about half of all teachers missed one step in solving the division problem. In the first sample, 927 had to be divided by 9. Conceptually and in terms of notation, the confusing part for children is how to deal with 27. The divisor 9 exceeds the second digit of the dividend 2. Therefore, 0 will have to be written before dealing with the next digit, 7, of 27. From option 2 in both samples, we can see that is where the child has made a mistake. Hence, it is important to deal clearly with each step in the computation. Not showing all computational steps could result in children not acquiring fundamental concepts to be proficient in this competency area. In teacher training or in providing onsite support, it will be useful to reinforce the point that all steps should be clearly written down when

Table 3.3 Teachers' Ability to Solve Division Problem with Steps
percent

	Solved correctly	Solved incorrectly	No response	Total
Teachers who solved the division problem correctly	77.8	13.9	8.3	100
	All 3 steps correctly	*At least 2 steps shown*	*Less than 2 steps shown correctly*	
Teachers who showed steps correctly (of those who solved the problem correctly)	10.5	46.5	53.5	

teaching children how to solve problems. Even just following the methods in the textbooks and teacher guides would be a good idea.

Another example in the teacher questionnaire is that in Class V and Class VI, children are taught how to use operations and brackets, part of basic mathematical operations. (BODMAS[7] requires computation of multiple mathematical operations, such as division, multiplication, addition, and subtraction, which are given in brackets.) Teachers were shown a problem and the answers of four children. They needed to correct children's work and decide who had gotten the correct answer.

As in the previous tasks, approximately 80 percent of teachers marked the correct student's work as correct. Here, too, special strategy for training is needed for the 20 percent whose basic mathematical knowledge is weak.

Understanding What Children Know from Analyzing Their Mistakes

This task explored teachers' ability to learn from children's mistakes. A sample of a child's work is shown in figure 3.2. This is a very common mistake. Children can add single digit numbers but don't quite know what to do when there is a carryover. Here, the child has attempted to add two 2-digit numbers with a carryover. Seven statements were given. Based on the given example of a child's work, teachers were asked to circle the options that they thought were true. Four out of seven statements were true about the competencies of the child (what she or he can or cannot do). The teacher had to circle the options that were true. Grading was done on the basis of the options circled. In other words, could the teacher identify the four statements that were true?

Figure 3.2 Can Teachers Learn from Children's Mistakes?

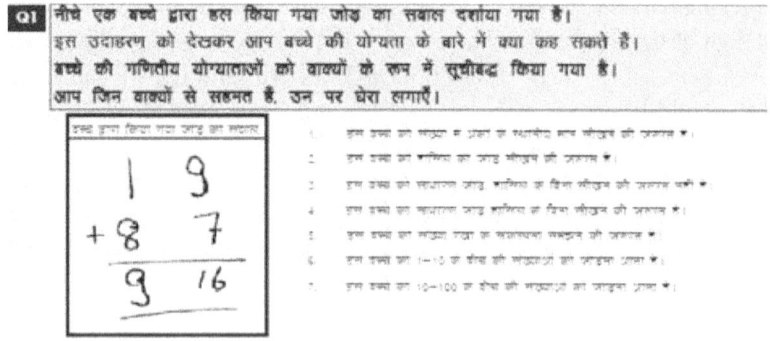

Translated into English, the seven statements read as follows:
  This child
   1. Needs to learn place value with numerals.
   2. Needs to learn addition with carryover.
   3. Does not need to learn simple addition without carryover.
   4. Needs to learn simple addition without carryover.
   5. Needs to get a conceptual understanding of the number line.
   6. Knows how to add numbers between 1 and 10.
   7. Knows how to add numbers between 10 and 100.
Four of the seven statements are true: 1, 2, 3, and 6.

Table 3.4 Teachers' Ability to Identify Correct Statements about Children's Work

Number of statements identified correctly by teachers	%
0 out of 4	20.4
1 out of 4	47.1
2 out of 4	10.7
3 out of 4	6.7
4 out of 4	2.3
No response	12.6
Total	**100**

What proportion of teachers could identify the true statements about the child's work? Table 3.4 shows how teachers dealt with this question. Less than 3 percent were able to identify all four true statements, and at least half the teachers identified at least one true statement.

Concrete examples such as the sample of a child's work, as shown in figure 3.2, are rarely discussed in teachers' trainings in India. And yet these are the realities of classrooms in primary grades and need to be dealt with practically. Looking at the distribution of scores for this item, it is possible that the instructions were misinterpreted; respondents may have thought that only one option needed to be circled. Still, it would be beneficial to use these kinds of tasks in future efforts in exploring what teachers think and what they can do.

One of the key elements of teaching is to look closely at the work that children are doing. Their mistakes provide important clues for what needs to be taught or reinforced. The ability to learn from children's work is an important ones. A good teacher will ensure that most of the children in his or her charge have understood the concepts or skills that are being taught before moving ahead. If teachers are unable to identify the gaps in their children's learning or abilities, then it is likely that not much can be done to help them before moving ahead to progressively harder concepts or skills. Carefully looking at children's work may be one way in which children can be prevented from getting left behind. And as outlined earlier, these are the kinds of skills needed if we are to depend on teachers to do comprehensive continuous evaluations (CCEs), and if CCE is to be the main mechanism for connecting assessment to instruction.

Explaining Processes and Solving Problems
Effective teaching has many dimensions. One essential activity is to explain a process clearly and correctly. The best way to judge how well a teacher is able to explain is to be in the classroom observing the instructor over a period of time. But this would require very skilled observers and graders and much more time. For this study, we wanted to get a sense of teachers' current ability to explain basic mathematical processes commonly used in elementary school classrooms. We wanted to do this on scale (about 2,200 teachers), so we resorted to a pen

and paper exercise where the teachers wrote explanations step by step. We used a variety of topics and types of formats for questions to do this. Topics included the following:

- Use of operations and brackets—BODMAS (numerical computation)
- Percentage problems (word problems)
- Area problem (word problem)

In some cases, examples were given, and in other cases they were not. But in all cases, there were precise instructions about writing the process step by step in the right sequence and clearly. What to write was also specified. Examples were given if we wanted teachers to write formulas, units, statements, and mathematical operations.

Ability to Do and Explain Numerical Mathematical Operations: BODMAS

This task has two parts. The first part assesses the ability of the teacher to carry out the BODMAS; 80 percent of teachers got the correct answer. The second part requires them to lay out the steps clearly (see figure 3.3). It is expected that students in Class V and Class VI will be able to solve these types of problems.

Teachers' work was graded in the following way (figure 3.4):

- Did the teacher solve the BODMAS problem correctly? (Was the final answer correct?)
- Did the teacher show all necessary steps in sequence with the correct mathematical operations? (Four steps needed to be shown.)

Figure 3.3 Sample Incorrect Response: Do Teachers Know BODMAS?

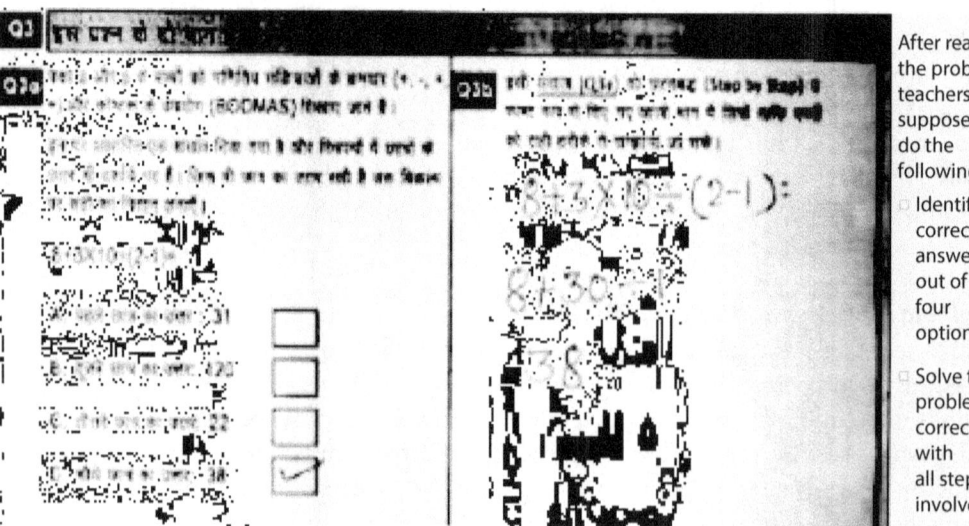

Note: BODMAS = Brackets, Orders (powers and roots), Division and Multiplication, Addition, and Subtraction.

Figure 3.4 Sample Correct Response: Do Teachers Know BODMAS?

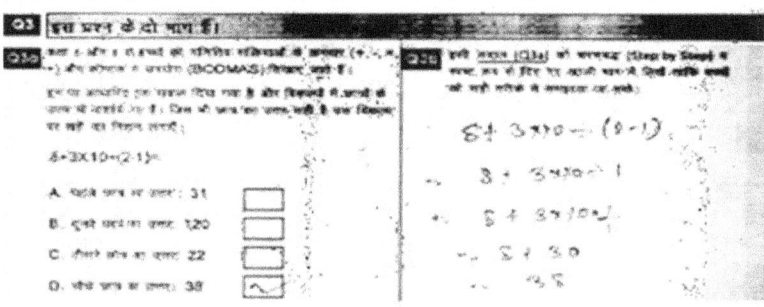

Note: BODMAS = Brackets, Orders (powers and roots), Division and Multiplication, Addition, and Subtraction.

Table 3.5 Teachers' Ability to Solve Step-by-Step Process of Numerical Computation (BODMAS)

	%
Solved correctly (final answer is correct)	74.7
Solved incorrectly	7.4
No response	17.9
Total	100
Of those who got the answer correct, teachers who showed steps showed...	
All 4 steps correct	78.8
At least 3 steps correct	86.5

Note: BODMAS = Brackets, Orders (powers and roots), Division and Multiplication, Addition, and Subtraction.

The content area (BODMAS) assessed in this task is part of the upper primary curriculum. Most teachers were able to provide the correct answer and were able to show the necessary mathematical steps to arrive at the correct answer (table 3.5). During teacher training, it is important to identify and help those who cannot do such operations.

Ability to Solve Word Problems and Show the Process of Solving Step by Step: Perimeter

The problem-solving template was divided into three sections (see figure 3.5): one section to write the formulas; another section to write the final correct answer; and a final section to write the mathematical processes and explanations. The teachers had to write the formulas that were used to solve the problem, solve the problem, and lay out each of the steps in sequence. The steps had to include descriptive statements and mathematical operations.

Figure 3.5 Sample Correct Response: Can Teachers Show How to Do Calculations for Perimeter?

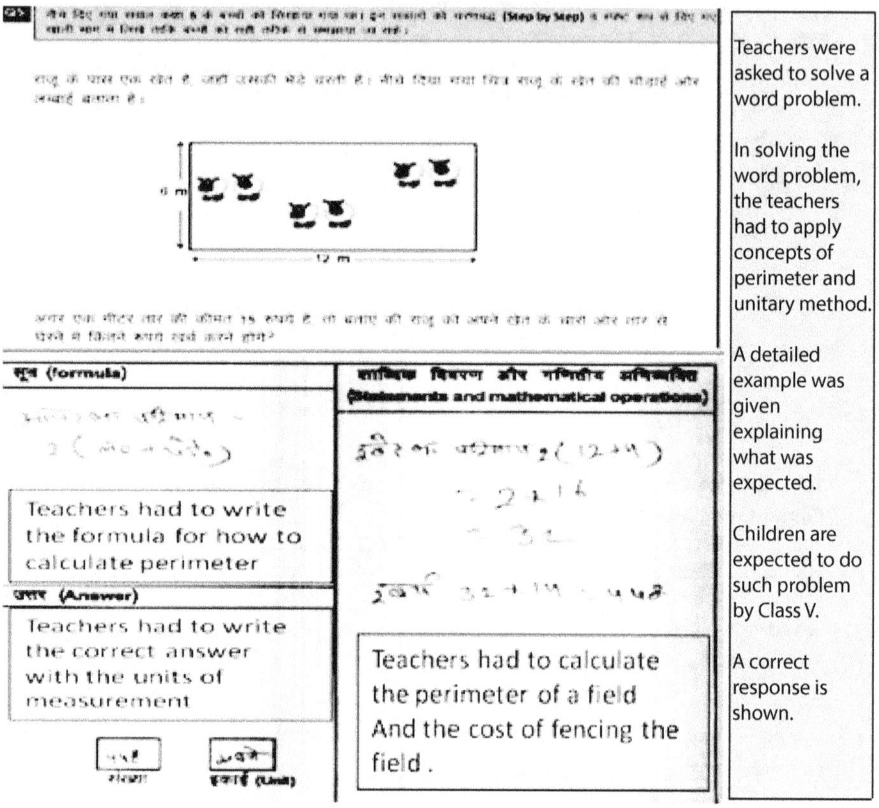

Teachers were asked to solve a word problem.

In solving the word problem, the teachers had to apply concepts of perimeter and unitary method.

A detailed example was given explaining what was expected.

Children are expected to do such problem by Class V.

A correct response is shown.

Teachers had to write the formula for how to calculate perimeter

Teachers had to write the correct answer with the units of measurement

Teachers had to calculate the perimeter of a field And the cost of fencing the field.

Teachers' work was graded as follows:

- Did the teacher use the correct formula for perimeter?
- Was the teacher able to solve the problem correctly? (Was the final answer and the unit of measurement correct?)
- Could the teacher solve and explain the two parts of the problem correctly? (Did the teacher find the perimeter of the field and the cost for fencing it?)

The first noticeable pattern is that almost one-fourth of all teachers did not respond to this question (table 3.6). While it is not easy to interpret the meaning of this missing data, it is likely that respondents found the question difficult. For each of the distinct tasks that were laid out, only about one-third of all teachers were able to do it correctly and completely. It is worrying that the final answer was not correct for such a large section of teachers. The percentage of respondents who got the correct and complete answer and showed all steps systematically was quite low, at 12 percent.

Table 3.6 Teachers' Ability to Solve Perimeter Problem Step by Step and in Sequence
percent

	Correct	Incorrect or incomplete	No response	Total
Number in the final answer	38.6	36.5	24.8	100
Unit in the final answer	37.1	34.4	28.6	100
Final answer (correct number and correct unit)	33.5	41.9	28.6	100
All steps written correctly and final answer correct	12.3	76.3	11.4	100

The content area (mensuration) assessed in this task is part of the upper primary curriculum and is an important competency. Do the data in table 3.6 indicate that many teachers may lack sufficient knowledge of upper primary math concepts? The findings certainly support the hypothesis that a substantial proportion of teachers need to be oriented toward how to show steps in solving problems so that children can understand and learn.

Ability to Solve Word Problems and Show the Process of Solving Step by Step: Percentages

By the time students reach Class V and VI, it is expected that they will be able to solve word problems that require percentage calculations and use of the unitary method. Percentages are also needed in everyday calculations, so such computations are used routinely. Therefore, teachers should be able to do them and show students how such problems are solved.

The actual question included in the teacher questionnaire is the following: "48 students are enrolled in one class. Today 36 students are present. What percentage of students is absent?" (see figure 3.6).[8] Such calculations should be a part of the daily life of the school.

The problem can be solved in two steps. First, calculate the number of children absent; second, work out the percentage of children who are absent. The teachers were expected to write the appropriate statements and do the mathematical calculations arriving at the correct answer. This procedure is laid out in detail in the textbooks.

Teachers' work was graded in the following way:

- Did the teacher get the correct answer to each part?
- Did the teacher write all descriptive statements?
- Did the teacher show all mathematical computations correctly?

Let us see how the teachers fared with the percentages (see table 3.7). While about two-thirds of all teachers got the correct final answer, most teachers did not write down all steps in a systematic way. Again this gap can easily be addressed in teacher training and through onsite support.

Here are some samples of teachers' work (figure 3.6).

Figure 3.6 Sample Response: Can Teachers Show How a Percentage Problem Is to Be Done?

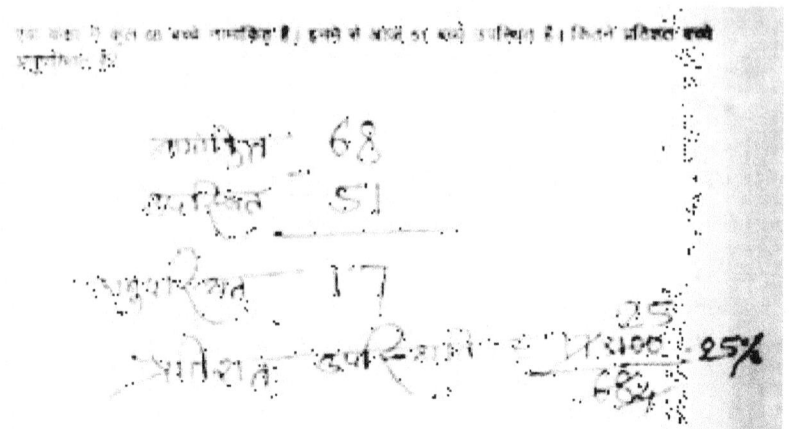

In this example, the teacher has worked out the final answer correctly, but has not shown the statements or the steps clearly.

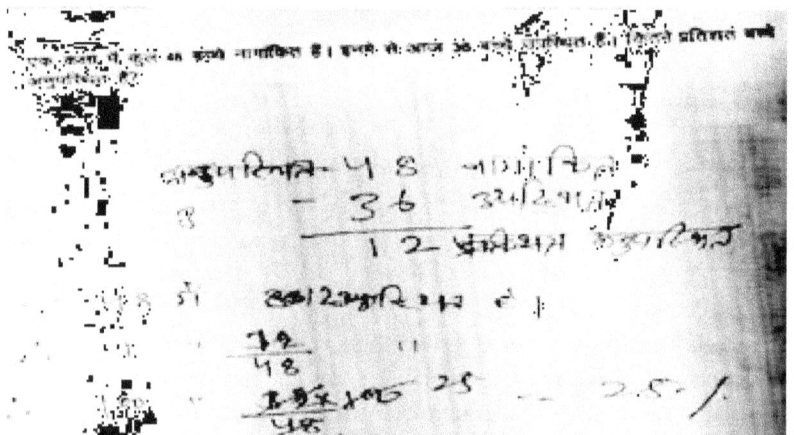

In this example, the teacher has worked out the final answer, but the steps are not clear.

Table 3.7 Teachers' Ability to Solve Percentage Problem Step by Step and in Sequence
percent

	Correct	Incorrect	No response	Total
Final answer	64.1	16.1	19.8	100
Final answer with steps and computations (in both parts) written down	37.1	28.9	33.8	100
Final answer and all steps (including mathematical statements and computations)	15.1	51.1	33.5	100

Those who could not solve the problem (regardless of whether they could write down the steps or not) are a source of concern. Having one out of every three teachers unable to solve such a problem is not a good situation. How to identify such teachers as early as possible and give them extra attention are issues that need to be addressed.

Developing Questions for Children Based on Context

The National Curriculum Framework of Teacher Education (NCFTE) and the Bihar Curriculum Framework (BCF) suggest that the everyday lives of children should be connected to what goes on in the classroom. One way is by teachers creating contextually relevant problems for children to tackle. Further, if CCE is to be taken as a guiding principle for teaching and learning and for classroom transactions, then a teacher should be able to tailor what is done in the classroom based on what the children are able to do and develop assessment tasks accordingly.

Creativity, flexibility, and the ability of creating contextually relevant tasks were assessed by asking teachers to develop questions and problems for children based on a set of instructions. The task is shown in figure 3.7.

The teachers had to develop a math word problem using three numbers and two mathematical operations. Further, the teachers could not use numbers or mathematical operations other than the ones provided. In addition, the context of the question and the vocabulary should be familiar so that students can comprehend them.

Teachers' work was graded in the following way:

- Mathematical appropriateness: Did the teachers use only the given numbers and the mentioned mathematical operations (addition and subtraction)?
- Logical and practical: Was the scenario for the word problem realistic and logical?

Some examples of teachers' work are shown in figures 3.8–3.10.

Teachers seem to have difficulty in generating their own word problems. A substantial number of teachers did not attempt this question. Although some teachers could develop word problems that were mathematically appropriate, logical, and practical, many struggled.

Interpreting Data

Data representation and interpretation of data from tables and other visual material are becoming increasingly important in math classrooms, especially in

Figure 3.7 Developing Questions for Children Based on Context

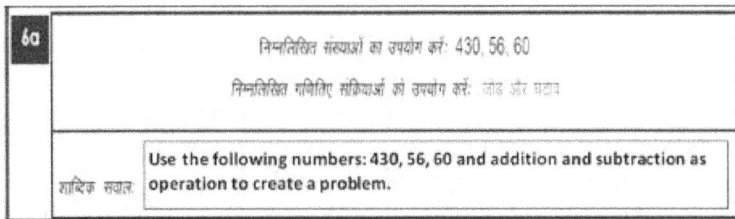

Figure 3.8 Sample Incorrect Response: Teacher Does Not Use Mathematical Operations

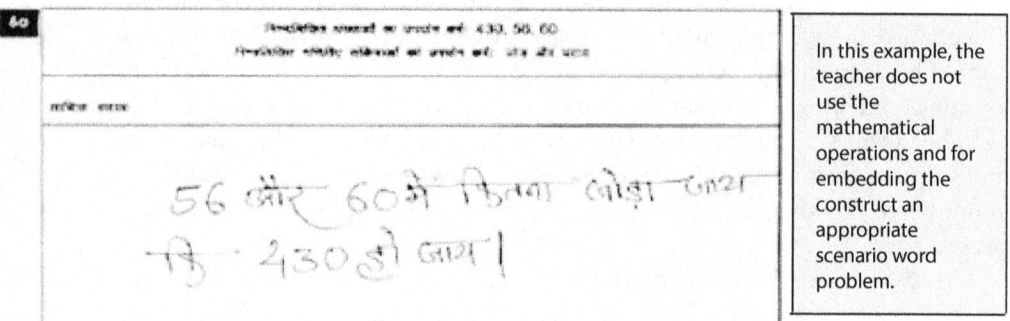

In this example, the teacher does not use the mathematical operations and for embedding the construct an appropriate scenario word problem.

Figure 3.9 Sample Incorrect Response: Teacher Is Unable to Construct a Logical and Realistic Scenario

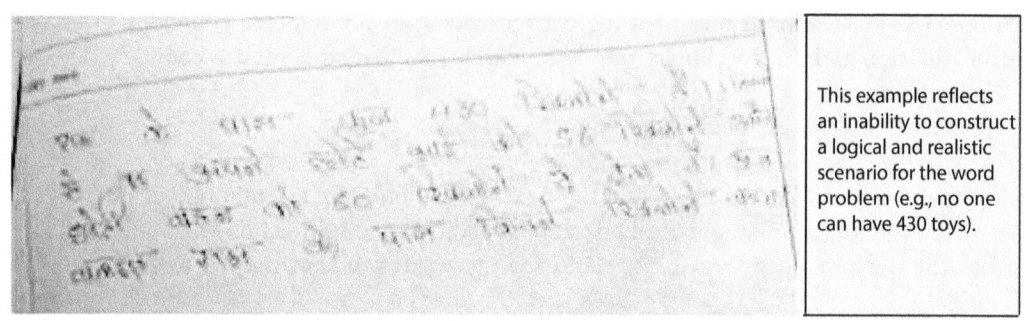

This example reflects an inability to construct a logical and realistic scenario for the word problem (e.g., no one can have 430 toys).

Figure 3.10 Sample Incorrect Response: Teacher Uses Mathematically Inappropriate Numbers

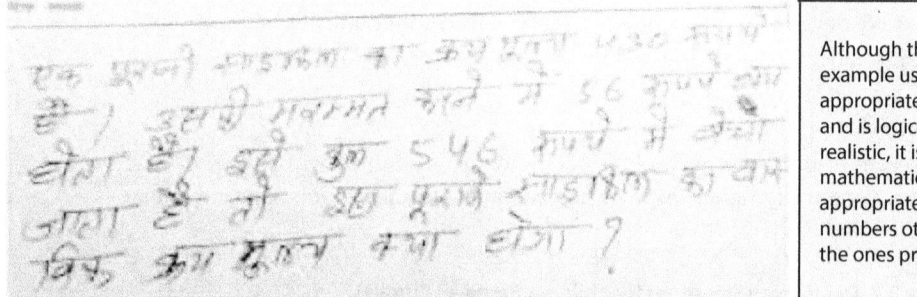

Although this example uses an appropriate scenario and is logical and realistic, it is not mathematically appropriate. It uses numbers other than the ones provided.

middle school. It is common to see such content in textbooks and in assessments. One such task was given to teachers in the teacher assessment. A table with information about population in four villages was presented (figure 3.11). The data include figures on total male, female, and child population.

The problem has five subquestions. To answer the questions, the data in the table has to be understood, interpreted, and applied. Teachers' work was graded in the following way: Did the teacher get the correct answer to each subquestion?

Figure 3.11 Data Table and Interpretation Task

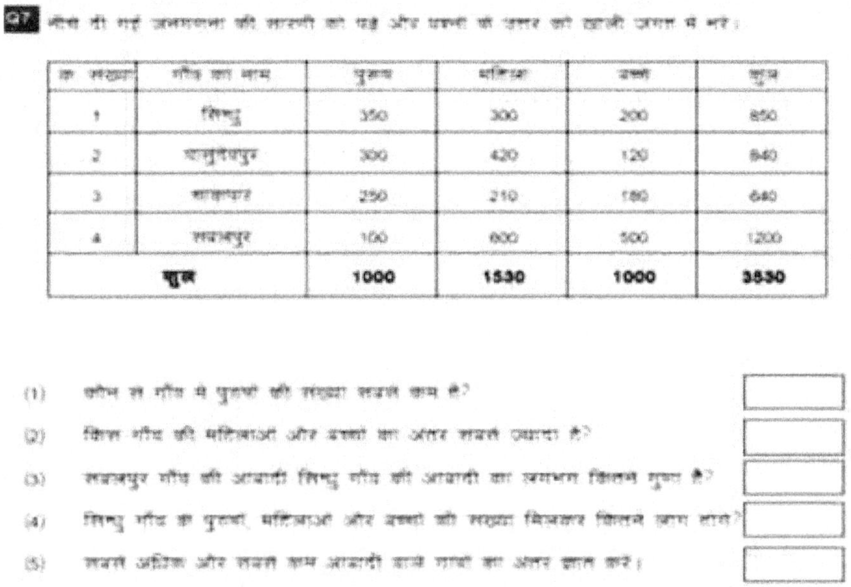

[Figure showing a data table in Hindi with columns for गाँव का नाम, पुरुष, महिला, बच्चे, कुल, and 5 interpretation subquestions with answer boxes]

Table 3.8 Teachers' Ability to Complete Data Interpretation Task Correctly

No. of correct answers, out of 5	Percent
0	0.7
1	2.9
2	6.3
3	12.0
4	24.8
5	48.5
No response	4.9
Total	100

Nearly half of the teachers answered all subquestions correctly (see table 3.8). Another 25 percent could answer four out of five subquestions correctly. This implies that for the remainder—25 percent of teachers—activities related to data interpretation and application were a problem. In today's world, the ability to make sense of information is becoming increasingly important. Within the domain of data handling, understanding of data in a table is a basic skill. Not only are children supposed to be able to use data in middle school, but teachers need to be adept at handling data in their regular work.

Concluding Thoughts for Math Teaching

Looking at the findings of the math section in the context of the assessment framework, here are some considerations in training teachers or in providing onsite support.

Understanding Children's Mistakes
Most teachers can spot when children are doing things wrong (see division problem, two-digit addition problem), but fewer can use children's work as a basis for explaining or teaching or using a different pedagogical approach. In any future orientation of teachers, it is essential that they are taught how to pay attention to and learn from children's work. This practice could prevent children from getting left behind and give teachers continuous clues about how to reinforce or review what they are teaching and how they are teaching.

Explaining Procedures
A large proportion of teachers can solve problems (content knowledge), but fewer can lay out the steps clearly to explain the process of how to reach the right answer. Such processes are clearly laid out in the textbook and can be followed by teachers. Being able to explain clearly and systematically is a vital part of good teaching. While it is obviously important that teachers have subject matter knowledge and skill, these skills cannot help children learn unless teachers are able to explain subjects well.

Generating Problems
Generating problems and problem sums is what the teachers find the hardest to do. Yet, looking at principles laid out in NCFTE and the Bihar Curriculum Framework (BCF), the ability to generate problems is critical to the pedagogical process as it is for meeting the requirements of CCE. It is therefore it is essential to develop this kind of skill among teachers.

Teacher Questionnaire and Teacher Assessment: Language

Conceptually, the framework for assessment for understanding how teachers teach language (Hindi) is designed to be similar to that used for teaching math. Here, too, there are three broad domains: understanding children's work and correcting children's written work; explaining and summarizing; and developing questions for children in the context of their conditions (table 3.9). As in math, tasks are designed such that they closely mirror types of teaching activities commonly seen or should be seen in elementary school classrooms.

Table 3.9 Framework for Assessment of Teaching of Language (Hindi)

Serial number	Domains	Description of items and tasks
1	Understanding and correcting children's work	Items assess the ability of teachers to understand and correct some of the common mistakes made by children.
2	Explaining and summarizing	Items assess the teacher's ability to read, comprehend, and write using appropriate vocabulary and language (which can be easily understood by children).
3	Developing questions keeping in mind contextual conditions	Items assess the teacher's ability to create questions based on a text that can be meaningfully understood by children.

Understanding and Correcting Children's Work

Here we have used three categories of tasks for understanding and correcting children's work. These include grammar and sentence construction, punctuation, and reading comprehension. These were relatively easy to do in a questionnaire format in which teachers did the tasks in a self-reported form with pen and paper.

Understanding and Correcting Children's Work: Grammar and Sentence Construction

Conventions of using language include domains such as grammar and sentence construction. One aspect of teaching language is to ensure that children develop strong language usage skills. One of the first tasks on the questionnaire was to correct several sentences that children had written (figure 3.12).

This assessment task had three subquestions. In each subquestion, a child-written sentence was given that had different types of mistakes. These mistakes could be of spelling, gender, singular or plural, or tense. The teacher had to do the following: (a) circle the mistakes made by the child in the given sentence, (b) identify the types of mistakes made by the child, and (c) rewrite the sentence correctly.

Teachers work was graded in the following way:

- Did the teacher attempt the task?
- Did the teacher identify all the mistakes in the sentence?
- Did the teacher correctly identify the type of mistake?
- Did the teacher rewrite the sentence correctly?

Table 3.10 gives an example of how teachers have corrected grammar in children's work in one of the subsections of the questionnaire.

Figure 3.12 Do Teachers Know Grammar?

Can they identify commonly made grammatical mistakes?
Can they correctly rewrite a grammatically incorrect sentence?

Teachers were asked to read a sentence written by a child. See example below.

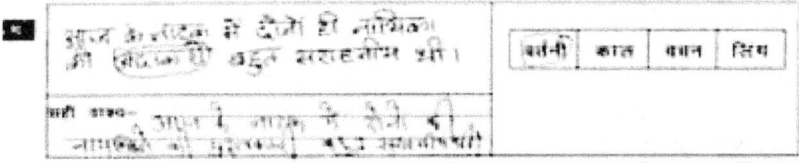

After reading the sentence, written by a child, teachers were asked to:
- Circle the mistakes made by the child
- Identify the types of mistakes made by the child—mistakes could be of tense, singular/plural, masculine/feminine, and spellings.
- Rewrite the sentence correctly

One example was provided to illustrate how to answer the question.

Three such subquestions were given. In each, four types of possible mistakes could be marked.

Table 3.10 Teachers' Ability to Correct Children's Mistakes: Grammar and Sentence Construction
percent

	Teachers who can identify the type of mistakes the child made	Teachers who can rewrite the sentence with correct grammar
Incorrect	69.2	59.3
Correct	27.8	35.9
No response	2.9	4.9
Total	100	100

Note: Teachers' response for the exercise in figure 3.12.

Table 3.11 Teachers' Ability to Correct Children's Grammar and Sentence Construction
percent

	Teachers who can identify the type of mistakes the child made	Teachers who can rewrite the sentence with correct grammar
Very good (3 correct out of 3)	1.3	20.2
Average (2 correct out of 3)	18.0	26.6
Below average (1 correct out of 3)	45.9	23.3
Very poor (none correct out of 3)	33.5	27.2
No response	1.3	2.7
Total	100	100

Note: Teacher performance in all three subsections of correcting grammar and sentence construction.

The aforementioned data provide insight into the basic teacher competencies of grammar and spelling, which are foundations of language learning. Clearly, a large proportion of teachers were not able to identify the mistakes or categorize them (table 3.11). Also, when teachers wrote the corrected sentence, it was clear that many were below par in their knowledge of grammar and spelling. About 20 percent of all teachers who completed the questionnaire (approximately 2,200) were able to write all three sentences with correct grammar and sentence construction.

Understanding and Correcting Children's Punctuation

If you open the notebook of any child in primary school or even in the upper primary grades and look at his or her written work, one of the most visible and noticeable things that jumps out is the lack of punctuation. The task discussed in this section assesses teacher's knowledge of punctuation—his or her ability to find the child's mistake and correct it. A sentence is given and the teacher has to write a correct version of the sentence (figure 3.13).

Table 3.12 shows the data for all teachers for this subquestion and indicates that well over half of all teachers were not able to write the corrected sentence with the appropriate punctuation.

Table 3.13 summarizes teachers' responses in correcting punctuation.

Figure 3.13 Sample Response: Punctuation Question

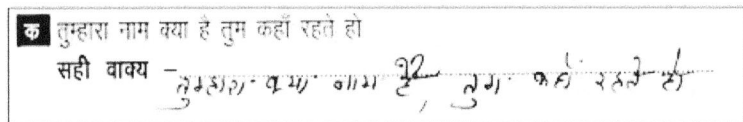

Correct Answer

तुम्हारा नाम क्या है? तुम कहाँ रहते हो (Two question marks needed to be inserted).

Table 3.12 Teachers' Ability to Correct Children's Mistakes: Punctuation

Teachers rewriting the sentence with correct punctuation marks[a]	Percent
Incorrect	56.6
Correct	35.5
No response	7.8
Total	100

a. Teachers' response for the question in figure 3.13.

Table 3.13 Teachers' Ability to Correct Children's Mistakes: Punctuation

Teachers rewriting the sentence with correct punctuation marks[a]	Percent
Very good (3 correct out of 3)	1.5
Average (2 correct out of 3)	25.6
Below average (1 correct out of 3)	42.6
Very poor (none correct out of 3)	27.3
No response	2.9
Total	100

a. Putting together teachers' responses in all three subsections of the question.

Like grammar and sentence construction, punctuation is a basic building block of the written form of language. The data suggest that either teachers' application of correct punctuation is weak, or they were not paying close attention to the questions asked in the survey. Only slightly more than one-fourth of all teachers were able to rewrite all or most sentences correctly.

Correcting Children's Work: Reading Comprehension

An extract of an informative text (at the Class V to Class VI level) was provided. Two multiple-choice questions followed the text. The first multiple-choice question was a direct fact retrieval question. To answer the question, the child could select the information directly from the text. The second question was an inference-based question. To answer the second question, the child had to interpret or make inferences about the information in the text. In the questionnaire, a child's work was used as a sample. The child had answered both questions by circling an option.

Figure 3.14 Sample Response: Correcting Children's Work: Reading Comprehension

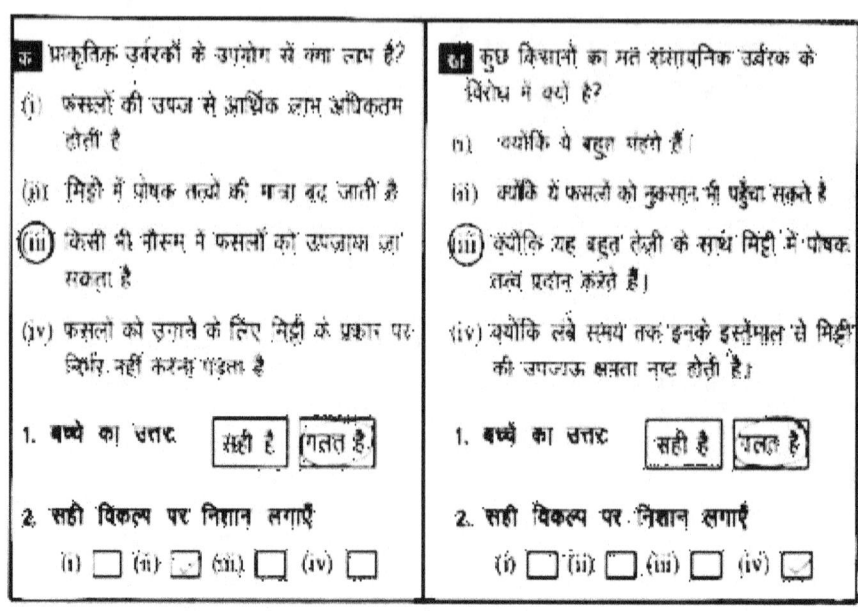

For the first question, the teacher correctly identified that the child's response was incorrect. And he or she himself or herself marked an incorrect option as the correct answer.

The instructions for the teachers were the following: "This text has been given to students of Class VI. There are two questions based on the text. See the response to these questions by one child. Please see what the child has done. Indicate whether the child has marked the correct option or not. Then tick the correct option." This set of tasks assesses the teachers' ability to read, comprehend, and correct children's work (see figure 3.14).

First, teachers had to note if the child had marked the correct answer or not. Then they were expected to tick the correct option for the same questions. Teachers' work was graded in the following way: (a) did the teacher correctly identify the child's response as correct or incorrect, (b) did the teacher identify the correct option for the questions?

About two-thirds of all teachers were able to correct the work of the given child correctly—both marking the child's work and pointing out the correct option. Those who could not do it correctly are a cause for concern (table 3.14).

Explaining Meaning of Words: Vocabulary

As students move through the primary and the middle school grades, the language and vocabulary in their textbooks become harder and more difficult

Table 3.14 Teachers' Ability to Correct Reading Comprehension Questions
percent

Teachers correcting children's work		Teachers marking options themselves	
Incorrectly identified child's work	33.2	Incorrect choice	37.9
Correctly identified child's work	63.6	Correct choice	58.9
No response	3.2	No response	3.2
Total	**100**	**Total**	**100**

Figure 3.15 Sample Response: Vocabulary

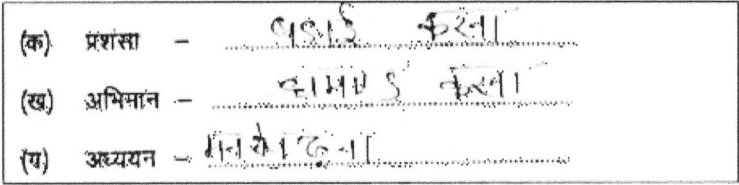

The teacher correctly gave easier words to explain the meaning of the given words.

Table 3.15 Teachers' Ability to Explain Difficult Words in Simple Language
percent

	Word a	Word b	Word c
Wrote the correct meaning	65.5	84.2	70.3
Wrote the incorrect meaning	27.1	9.5	22.7
Wrote the irrelevant meaning	0.5	0.5	0.5
No response	6.7	5.9	7.0
Total	**100**	**100**	**100**

to understand. This is true in language textbooks and probably even more so if we look at the content in other subjects. Therefore, it is important to ensure that teachers are able to explain difficult words in easy to understand ways.

This assessment task exploring teachers' ability to explain difficult words was based on three words chosen from Bihar textbooks (for grades 4 and 6). Teachers were expected to write the meanings of these words in simple language and sentences so children could understand them. Since this task is a common classroom practice that cuts across grades and subjects, it is important that teachers know how to explain and convey the meanings of difficult words in the textbooks (sample response in figure 3.15).

Table 3.15 outlines the response of teachers to each of the words separately, as the level of difficulty varied depending on the word.

Vocabulary acquisition is an important competency in children's language development and a critical component of content knowledge accumulation. In classroom practice, it is essential for teachers to be able to explain the meaning of difficult or unfamiliar words in a way using language accessible to children. A limited vocabulary might pose problems for children as they move to more complex competencies of language learning. The data suggest that a high proportion of teachers could write a clear definition of the given words. In pre-service or in-service teacher training, it could be possible to identify teachers who have limited vocabulary or are unable to explain difficult words. Such teachers can be given extra support.

Developing Original Questions Based on a Given Text

For any kind of classroom teaching, it is expected that textbook content will be supplemented with appropriate and contextual matter created by the teacher. Are teachers able to generate questions on a given text? This was explored in the questionnaire. This task assesses the ability of teachers to create questions that can be meaningfully understood by children based on a given text. For example, although one expects teachers to use texts from textbook chapters, they should also be able to develop questions that go beyond the questions in the textbooks.

Figure 3.16 Question Development Task

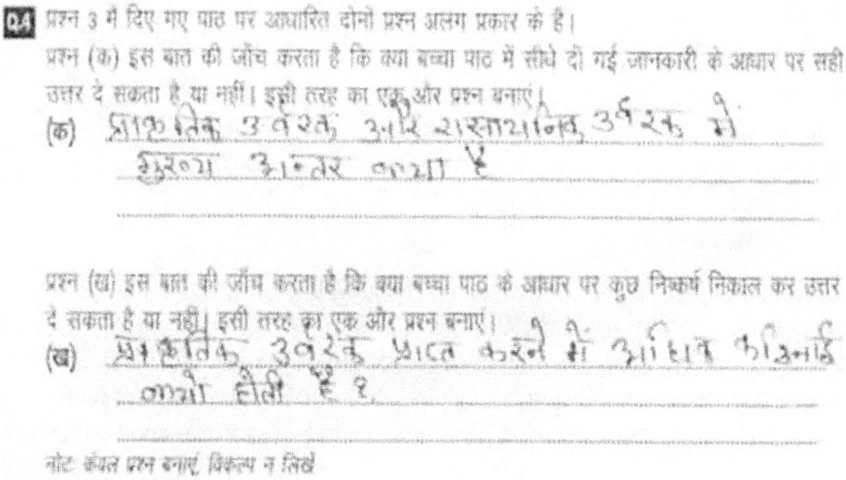

Q.4 प्रश्न 3 में दिए गए पाठ पर आधारित दोनों प्रश्न अलग प्रकार के हैं।

प्रश्न (क) इस बात की जाँच करता है कि क्या बच्चा पाठ में सीधे दी गई जानकारी के आधार पर सही उत्तर दे सकता है या नहीं। इसी तरह का एक और प्रश्न बनाएं।

(क) प्राकृतिक उर्वरक और रासायनिक उर्वरक में मुख्य अन्तर क्या है

प्रश्न (ख) इस बात की जाँच करता है कि क्या बच्चा पाठ के आधार पर कुछ निष्कर्ष निकाल कर उत्तर दे सकता है या नहीं। इसी तरह का एक और प्रश्न बनाएं।

(ख) प्राकृतिक उर्वरक प्राप्त करने में अधिक कठिनाई क्यों होती है?

नोट: केवल प्रश्न बनाएं, विकल्प न लिखें

The teacher develops both questions aligned to the requirements (clear, grade-appropriate, fact retrieval, and inference).

Table 3.16 Teachers' Ability to Create Clear and Appropriate Questions
percent

Response type	Direct retrieval questions (%)	Inference-based questions (%)
Correct response	39.1	33.3
Incorrect response	18.6	18.7
Irrelevant response	31.3	35.4
No response	11.0	12.6
Total	**100**	**100**

From the extract of an informative text, teachers had to develop two questions similar to the ones they answered earlier. Question 1 had to be a direct fact retrieval question. To answer the question, a child would be able to select the information directly from the text. Question 2 had to be an inference-based question (see sample response in figure 3.16). To answer the question, a child would have to interpret or make inferences about the information in the text.

Teachers' work was graded in the following way:

- Did the teacher develop a question that was clear? (In other words, what is being asked?)
- Was the developed question a fact retrieval or inference-based question?

Data on the ability to generate questions are interesting (table 3.16). About one-third of the teachers were able to develop questions, despite this being a relatively new kind of task for teachers. But a large proportion of teachers either did irrelevant or incorrect work. Of course, based on one item, it is difficult to interpret what the data indicate, but it is possible to hazard guesses. It is quite likely that teachers find it difficult to step outside the boundaries of the textbook. An obvious implication for preservice or in-service teacher training would be to discuss lessons in training sessions and put teachers through exercises of creating questions that relate to the subject and to the text but are not laid out in the textbook.

Summarizing

On any given day in school, one of the most common tasks in the classroom is summarizing and wrapping up what has been read or discussed in class. A good teacher should be able to do this easily. Of course, doing this task well requires teachers to read, comprehend, and summarize the main points using appropriate vocabulary that can be easily understood by children.

The teacher had to read a fictional text extracted from a children's story. Then she or he had to write an appropriate summary in simple words and in five sentences. In language teaching in primary grades or in middle school, it is a common practice to summarize what has been taught or read.

Table 3.17 Teachers' Ability to Summarize Content
percent

Summary with main points	
Less than or greater than 5 main relevant points	49.1
5 main relevant points	27.9
Irrelevant response	15.2
No response	7.8
Total	**100**
Summary with correct grammar	
2 or fewer than 2 mistakes	41.0
More than 2 mistakes	35.7
Irrelevant response	15.1
No response	8.3
Total	**100**

Teachers' work was graded in the following way:

- Did the summary cover five main points, and were the points in the right sequence?
- Was it largely written in the teachers' own words rather than from picked up sentences from the text?
- Was the summary free of grammatical and spelling mistakes (two or less)?

Summarizing content seems to be much more difficult for most teachers compared with other tasks, like explaining vocabulary or basic reading comprehension (table 3.17). About one-third of all teachers were able to write the summary in five relevant points with a proper beginning, middle, and ending. A substantial percentage of teachers did not even comprehend the task. Summarizing a story is an important competency and is required in the classroom almost daily.

Wrapping Up the Language Section of the Teacher Assessment Part of the Study

Looking at the data in the context of the assessment framework developed for language, here are some things to think about: teachers had fairly good content knowledge (see vocabulary tasks and reading comprehension), but the ability to translate that knowledge into meaningful explanations was weaker. Tasks that needed application, such as creating questions or summarizing, seemed to be harder. A substantial number of irrelevant responses indicate that teachers did not understand or take the assessment task seriously. Many of these issues can easily be tackled in teacher training and practiced either in the preservice phase or during in-service training opportunities.

Thoughts on a Way Forward

Before concluding this section on teacher assessment, we will reflect on the usefulness of this exercise and lay out some possibilities for how evidence can be used for future action.

Usefulness of the Teacher Assessment Exercise

The teacher assessment questionnaire was one part of a bigger study with many components. Therefore, this section could not be more extensive given the constraints of time and resources. From a statistical point of view, more items for each domain would have been desirable. But even with an hour and a half allotted to each subject questionnaire, teachers felt the assessment was too long. However, in the future if a similar exercise were to be undertaken, care could be given to having only this kind of questionnaire administered on a chosen day or during one visit. An important learning, which reinforces our previous experience, is that since the government had approved of this study, there was not much of a problem getting teachers to participate in the assessment. Any residual resistance from teachers was further diluted as a result of no names being required on the answer sheets. This assured teachers that no action would be taken against individuals.

The experience from presenting the preliminary results of this study to the different departments and levels of the state government indicates that there is a lot of interest in the tools and the findings of such an effort.[9] Further, since this is a baseline study, and since many more developments related to teacher professional development are planned in Bihar in the immediate future, focused dissemination and discussion activities are planned.

It has become common in India for different state governments to administer teacher eligibility tests (TETs) to all prospective teachers. TETs are high stakes pen and paper examinations that determine who gets a chance to qualify as a teacher. Most TETs are based on subject matter knowledge and on multiple-choice answers. Assessments like the ones in this study could be useful starting points to go deeper into and beyond subject matter knowledge and link it to teaching in a way that can directly influence how children gain from the educational experience. Even the frameworks used in this study are not considered to be appropriate for the TET context; such assessments could be adapted for use in the beginning and end of teacher training programs.

The process of grading is also worth discussion. Government representatives selected by SCERT participated in developing the rubrics for grading the teacher assessments in language and in math. This collaborative effort had significant benefits. For one, the learnings from the process of grading close to 4,500 answer sheets are immense. It was very useful that the same government representatives involved are also people who provide inputs into the development of state curriculum and textbooks and design teacher training content. In the future, more participation can be invited in such processes as a way of accelerating learning about what teachers need and of building capacities to deliver it.

In grading teacher responses and in presenting the findings, we find that the actual examples of teachers' work provide compelling evidence, especially for policy makers and practitioners.

To illustrate specific points in the report, we have provided numerous samples of teacher responses to different questions and tasks. However, it is worth thinking about how the vast accumulation of raw material (actual teacher papers) can be maximally and effectively used both as a "real" source of data and for more qualitative research for the future. It is also worth thinking about whether a sample of teachers' work should be digitized for tracking over time. All of this leads to thinking about the contours of a possible ongoing research program to accompany the next few years of action on teacher professional development.

Overall, in the context of this baseline study, the teacher assessment questionnaire provided insights about teachers' attitudes towards teaching practices. This data will enable links to be explored between what the teachers know and can potentially do with other characteristics.

Implications of This Evidence for Action

The teacher assessment section of the study provides inputs into teacher training programs for the future. In that sense, the aggregate data and the raw material of teacher answer sheets provide an invaluable source of insights. The study provides information on both the tools and the findings and together they have significant implications for strengthening and improving teaching in elementary grades.

First, the actual format in which tasks were presented in the teacher assessment questionnaire can be adapted easily for use with different topics and subjects in teacher training. For example, take the section on corrections. A collection of children's common mistakes in language and math can be incorporated into teacher training modules either in a worksheet form or as discussion items. Even the selection and collation of samples that highlight common mistakes by children will help bring a much-needed dose of reality from school classrooms into the classrooms of teacher training institutions. Children's work can also be used in online teacher training support materials. In addition, the basics of language, such as grammar, punctuation, spelling, and tense agreement, can be practiced easily by teachers identified as needing help in these areas. Correcting mistakes is one of the best ways to learn.

Second, the language and math surveys show that even if teachers have content knowledge, many are still weak at systematic and complete explanations of concepts and ideas. This calls for actual sessions in preservice and in-service training workshops where actual lessons can be read, discussed, and practiced. Group discussions of selected chapters from different subject textbooks of different grades help all teachers focus on the important content areas and the best ways to communicate key points to students. The vocabulary exercise from the questionnaire suggests that in workshops, teachers can identify hard words and provide explanations for them. If done in a group, such efforts build capacity, strengthen preparation for teaching, and can even help generate teacher-led, practice-based teaching guides.

Third, generating new questions and connecting textbooks content to everyday life was difficult for many teachers. Such activities need preparation, practice, and on-site support. In addition, others in the system, such as cluster coordinators or faculty of teacher training institutes, could be encouraged to try such activities in actual classrooms to model good practices that could be used by practicing teachers.

While this study concentrated on three broad domains of common teaching practices and used them in different ways to explore how teachers think, similar exercises with other domains and common practices can also be conducted. Such efforts can be collected and used as periodic activities for assessment or capacity building in a face-to-face teaching training context or for distance learning and open course design.

Notes

1. In 2007–08, Geeta Gandhi Kingdon and Rukmini Banerji used teacher assessments of this kind in a study of schools in Bihar and Uttar Pradesh. Supported by the Spencer Foundation, this study, "SchoolTELLS," provided useful insights into teaching across government primary schools and private schools in the two states. Subsequently, funded by UNICEF and supported by the Ministry of Human Resource Development (MHRD) and based on the experiences and learnings from SchoolTELLS, a larger study, "Inside Primary Schools," was carried out by the Annual Status of Education Report, MHRD Centre/Pratham, in 2010–11 (http://www.asercentre.org/p/62.html).
2. The fundamental premise of CCE, which is mandated in the right to education act, is based on the ability of teachers to be able to assess their children in a flexible and ongoing way.
3. In the design stage, there were detailed discussions with different officials of Bihar government, including SCERT and senior officials of the Bihar government's Department of Education, with World Bank staff and with other experts.
4. Apart from the teacher assessment questionnaire discussed in this section, teachers were asked questions about their background and beliefs. Given the length of the entire exercise (in terms of what a teacher was asked), the teacher assessment section is perhaps shorter than if only this section had been administered separately.
5. This question has two parts: one part is aligned with domain 1, which assesses the ability to understand children's mistakes, and the other part is aligned with domain 2, which assesses the ability to explain processes and solve problems. In the teacher questionnaire, an example was shown of how to solve, step by step, a 3-digit by 1-digit division problem.
6. For about 20 percent of teachers, even a basic competency like this one may be a problem. Such exercises can be used in preservice or in-service training. During training, such teachers need to be identified and given extra attention.

7. BODMAS refers to Brackets, Orders (powers and roots), Division and Multiplication, Addition, and Subtraction.
8. In sample 2 of the teacher questionnaire, the same problem has different numbers: "68 students are enrolled and 51 are present. So what percentage is absent?"
9. Shorter documents (such as policy briefs), translations in Hindi, and short one-day workshops may go a long way in helping a wide cross-section within the government and outside absorb the results.

CHAPTER 4

Generating Composite Scores for Teacher Capability for Teaching

Introduction

The teacher assessment instrument was administered to all teachers in the sampled schools in language and mathematics. This was done in the first visit. The questions in both assessments covered basic competencies that teachers routinely teach in elementary school classes. For example, the language assessment covered sentence construction, punctuation, vocabulary, and comprehension. Similarly, the math assessment had questions on long division, basic mathematical operations and ordering mathematical operations (BODMAS), word problems using percentage, area, and data representation and interpretation. The assessment was designed to measure various domains of teacher capabilities that affect their ability to teach well. In particular, the questions addressed the teachers' ability to spot common mistakes in children's work, their own subject knowledge and ability to solve the problems correctly, and their ability to do so showing all the required steps. This latter area is especially important—the teacher should not only know the material she or he is teaching, but also be able to communicate it in a way that children learn and retain the material. In addition, both assessments had questions that addressed the teachers' ability to take given information and use it to frame grade-appropriate and contextually relevant questions for their students.

Generating Composite Scores

A detailed analysis of the teacher assessment is given in previous sections of the report. In those sections, the analysis describes teachers' competency in each area for each of the domains included. However, for tracking purposes, it is often useful to have one indicator that can be tracked. Usually these indicators are composite scores of some kind. Although a single indicator is useful for tracking purposes, it also has its limitations.

First, a single number is useful to summarize the position of the indicator in relation to where it should be, but it does not say much about where exactly the problem is. It is clear that a teacher with a low score will need help to improve. However, the score by itself will not provide guidance for what needs to change to result in improvement over time. In fact, it is the detailed question-by-question analysis that can address the issue of what needs to change. Second, a composite score combines different variables or subindicators, which involves deciding how to weigh these individual variables in the final composite variables. It is difficult to justify discretionary weights; however, naïve weights[1] may be too simplistic. More complicated weights, for instance, derived using principal component analysis, make unraveling the composite more difficult and even more of a "black box," since the composite becomes harder to interpret.

Keeping these caveats in mind, a composite score based on teacher assessments in language and math was constructed. Apart from its potential usefulness in tracking, for our purposes it serves another useful end. A composite score is far easier to work with (as compared with the individual questions in the assessment) to check which teacher characteristics, if any, correlate to teacher competency.

In constructing the composite indicator, we had to decide which variables to include and how to weight them. As discussed previously, the questions in the teacher assessment addressed different domains, and within each domain different competencies were tested. For the purposes of generating a composite teacher score, we extracted only the subject knowledge subindicator from each question. This makes the score far easier to interpret. There can be no argument that teachers need to know the material they are supposed to teach. Each item was given equal weight when combining questions.[2] Tables 4.1 and 4.2 describe the variables and how they were combined for the language and the math assessments, respectively.

The language score lies along a scale of 0–10 and the math score 0–12. Table 4.3 presents the distribution of these scores for the teachers in the sample.

Table 4.1 Composition of Teacher Assessment Language Score

Question	Competency	Parts	Domain	Grading	Range
1	Sentence construction	3	Whether teacher could write the sentence correctly	0 if all 3 parts incorrect or 1 of 3 correct 1 if 2 of 3 correct 2 if all 3 correct	0–2
2	Punctuation	3	Whether teacher could write the sentence correctly with punctuation	0 if all 3 parts incorrect or 1 of 3 correct 1 if 2 of 3 correct	0–2
3	Comprehension	1	Whether teacher could answer the question based on the given text	0 if incorrect 1 if correct	0–1
4	Comprehension	2	Whether teacher could write grade-appropriate questions based on the given text in Q3	Dropped	

table continues next page

Table 4.1 Composition of Teacher Assessment Language Score *(continued)*

Question	Competency	Parts	Domain	Grading	Range
5	Vocabulary	3	Whether teacher could give the meaning of given words in simple language	0 if all 3 parts incorrect 1 if 1 of 3 correct 2 if 2 of 3 correct 3 if all 3 correct	0–3
6	Summarizing text	1	Whether teachers could summarize a given text giving 5 main points and with 2 or less grammatical mistakes	0 if neither main points nor grammatical mistakes 1 if either main points or grammatical mistakes 2 if both main points were covered and there were no grammatical mistakes	0–2

Table 4.2 Composition of Teacher Assessment Math Score

Question	Competency	Parts	Domain	Grading	Range
1	Addition with carryover	1	Whether teacher could deduce what a child knows by looking at a solved problem	Dropped	
2	Long division	3	Whether teacher could grade a child's work correctly	0 if incorrect and 1 if correct	0–3
			Whether teacher could solve the problem correctly	0 if incorrect and 1 if correct	
			Whether teacher could solve the problem correctly showing at least 2 of the 3 steps	0 if incorrect and 1 if correct	
3	BODMAS	3	Whether teacher could grade a child's work correctly	0 if incorrect and 1 if correct	0–3
			Whether teacher could solve the problem correctly	0 if incorrect and 1 if correct	
			Whether teacher could solve the problem correctly showing at least 3 of the 4 steps	0 if incorrect and 1 if correct	
4	Word problem using percentage (2 parts involving calculation of a number and then a percentage)	2	Whether teacher could solve both parts of the problem correctly	0 if incorrect and 1 if correct	0–2
			Whether teacher could solve both parts of the problem correctly showing all steps and computations	0 if incorrect and 1 if correct	
5	Word problem using perimeter	2	Whether teacher could solve the problem correctly	0 if incorrect and 1 if correct	0–2
			Whether teacher could solve the problem correctly showing all steps and computations	0 if incorrect and 1 if correct	
6	Addition and subtraction using numbers 1–1,000	1	Whether teacher could set an addition or subtraction problem using numbers between 1 and 1,000	Dropped	
7	Data representation and interpretation	5	Whether teacher could answer simple questions based on a data table	0 if less than 4 parts correct 1 if 4 of 5 correct	0–2

Note: BODMAS = brackets, orders (powers and roots), division, multiplication, addition, subtraction.

Table 4.3 Distribution of Composite Scores
percent

Score	Language	Math
0	4.22	3.22
1	5.49	4.22
2	8.57	4.99
3	13.78	5.49
4	17.14	5.35
5	17.45	7.57
6	15.23	9.43
7	10.92	11.11
8	4.67	12.47
9	1.77	10.20
10	0.23	10.74
11	—	8.30
12	—	6.80
No response	0.54	0.14
No.	2,206	2,206
Mean	4.46	6.97
Median	5	7

Note: — = not available.

A total of 2,206 teachers participated in the assessment. The mean language score is 4.46, which is less than 50 percent. The mean math score is higher, at 7 out of a maximum of 12.

The questions in the assessment were at the level of standard (or grade) 4–6. Yet, less than 1 percent of teachers could score full points in the language assessment. The comparable number for math was higher, at 7 percent.

Teacher Characteristics and Composite Scores

Do teacher scores vary systematically with teacher characteristics? This section takes a quick look at some of the teacher background characteristics and how these vary (or not) with teacher scores.

In our sample, about 60 percent of the teachers are male, and 40 percent are female. Table 4.4 shows that male teachers are likely to have slightly higher mean scores than female teachers.

Table 4.5 suggests that general category teachers and those who are of Other Backward Classes have higher scores than teachers coming from a Scheduled Caste or Scheduled Tribe background.

Teachers with postgraduate educational qualifications do better than others. But even for them, the scores are not close to maximum by any means (table 4.6). And teachers with a Bachelor in Education degree seem to do slightly better than the other categories (table 4.7).[3]

Table 4.4 Teacher Scores, by Gender

Teacher gender	Teachers, by gender (%)	Average Hindi score	Average math score
Male	60.11	4.66	7.44
Female	39.89	4.15	6.25
Total	**100**	**4.46**	**6.97**

Table 4.5 Teacher Scores, by Caste

Teacher caste	Teachers, by category (%)	Average Hindi score	Average math score
General	26.90	4.72	7.20
Scheduled Castes	14.98	4.14	6.37
Scheduled Tribes	4.40	4.14	6.62
Other Backward Classes	53.49	4.44	7.04
Other	0.22	3.60	7.80
Total	**100**	**4.46**	**6.97**

Table 4.6 Teacher Scores, by Education Category

Teacher education	Teachers, by category (%)	Average Hindi score	Average math score
Class X	6.58	4.29	6.50
10+2 years	45.15	3.93	6.28
Graduate	32.52	4.87	7.48
Postgraduate	15.70	5.16	8.05
Total	**100**	**4.46**	**6.97**

Table 4.7 Teacher Scores, by Professional Qualifications

Teacher professional education	Teachers, by category (%)	Average Hindi score	Average math score
None	50.18	4.19	6.51
Diploma[a]	14.16	4.40	6.75
BEd	9.73	5.17	7.91
MEd	0.72	4.06	7.50
Other	25.20	4.79	7.62
Total	**100**	**4.46**	**6.97**

a. Diploma in elementary education, which qualifies teachers to teach Classes I through VIII.

It is interesting that the relation between teacher scores and years of teaching experience seems to have a U-shaped pattern, with the least experienced and most experienced teachers getting the highest scores, relatively speaking (table 4.8).

Those who taught previously in private schools (about 15 percent of the sampled teachers) seem to have a slight advantage in scores (table 4.9).

Table 4.8 Teacher Scores, by Years of Experience as Teacher

Years of being a teacher	Teachers, by category (%)	Average Hindi score	Average math score
0	8.31	5.53	8.74
1–2	8.09	4.36	6.75
3–5	14.36	3.95	6.04
6	10.49	3.91	5.92
7	10.18	4.22	6.29
8	23.74	4.46	7.20
9–10	10.40	4.41	7.13
>10	14.41	5.03	7.72
Total	100	4.46	6.97

Table 4.9 Teacher Scores, by Whether They Have Taught in a Private School in the Past

Previously taught in a private school	Teachers by category (%)	Average Hindi score	Average math score
Yes	15.39	4.85	7.78
No	84.61	4.39	6.82
Total	100	4.46	6.97

Looking Ahead

This study (data collection from all three visits combined) is a baseline glimpse of teachers and teaching in Bihar. It is expected that in the coming years there will be a sustained effort to strengthen teacher training institutions and a great deal of investment in building the professional capacity of teachers in the state. The big question facing Bihar will be gauging how much teachers and teaching have changed.

The present study needs to be expanded to generate deeper insights for planning ahead and remediation strategies to be put in place. It is important to explore what role the composite scores can or should play in understanding the "value added" in terms of outcomes in the years ahead. Some key issues related to these composite scores will be addressed as the project in the state moves to its next level.

The present elements need to be refined and expanded to subsequently gauge the change in teacher performance in the next few years. The teacher assessment framework is part of a larger study of teaching and learning that will provide inputs on the progress on teacher knowledge and skills as the project gains momentum. The team proposes to undertake a midline and an endline study with the composite scores refined to provide richer, usable data that will lead to focused policy action on teacher education reform.

To be able to compare the baseline to later periods (midline or endline), the common measures used in this study to construct the composite scores will be used as the indicators. The team recognizes the challenge of maintaining comparability and consistency to quantify change as it happens in the teacher education sector in the next few years.

As teacher training institutions become fully functional and preservice and in-service training and professional development activities are in full swing, it will be useful to revisit the issue of teachers and teaching in Bihar and conceptualize how the changes over time can be tracked and evaluated.

Notes

1. Equal weight for all the variables.
2. This weighting scheme results in questions that have more parts having a higher weight. However, this is preferable to assigning discretionary weights.
3. This will need to be checked further to see whether these are statistically significant differences.

Environmental Benefits Statement

The World Bank Group is committed to reducing its environmental footprint. In support of this commitment, the Publishing and Knowledge Division leverages electronic publishing options and print-on-demand technology, which is located in regional hubs worldwide. Together, these initiatives enable print runs to be lowered and shipping distances decreased, resulting in reduced paper consumption, chemical use, greenhouse gas emissions, and waste.

The Publishing and Knowledge Division follows the recommended standards for paper use set by the Green Press Initiative. Whenever possible, books are printed on 50 percent to 100 percent postconsumer recycled paper, and at least 50 percent of the fiber in our book paper is either unbleached or bleached using Totally Chlorine Free (TCF), Processed Chlorine Free (PCF), or Enhanced Elemental Chlorine Free (EECF) processes.

More information about the Bank's environmental philosophy can be found at http://crinfo.worldbank.org/wbcrinfo/node/4.

www.ingramcontent.com/pod-product-compliance
Lightning Source LLC
Chambersburg PA
CBHW080742250426
43671CB00038B/2843